Kenneth Copeland Ministries

Presents this Special Partner Edition of

Real People. Real Needs. Real Victories.

to

_____

on this day of _____ 19_____,

to commemorate our Covenant of Partnership
together. Gloria and I are committed to minister to you,
to pray for you every day, and to continue teaching you the
uncompromised Word of God that you may continue to
grow and increase in His anointing.
We stand with you in faith, and we love you.

Kenneth Copeland

Real People.

Real Needs.

Real Victories.

SPECIAL PARTNER EDITION

Kenneth Copeland Publications
Fort Worth Texas

Real People. Real Needs. Real Victories.

ISBN 1-57562-095-2　　　　　　　　　　　　30-0704

©1996 Kenneth Copeland Publications

All scripture is from the *King James Version* unless otherwise noted.

Kenneth Copeland Publications
Fort Worth, Texas 76192-0001

Table of Contents

Introduction by Gloria Copeland i

Chapter 1 **Testimonies of Faith** 1

Faith in Bloom 2

From Hart to Hearts 8

The Final Decree 15

Chapter 2 **Testimonies of Protection** 23

A Path Through Mighty Waters 24

Code Name: Prayer 33

When the Earth Shakes 41

Chapter 3 **Testimonies of Healing** 51

No Petal in Heaven's Garden 52

Countdown to a Miracle 62

A Lifetime Guarantee 70

In the Midst of the Cloud 79

Reaching Out for the Father's Hand . . . 87

Keeping the Promise in Sight 95

My God Can Turn It Around! 102

Tiny Warrior 110

*The Miraculous "Mending" of
    Jessica Salvage* 115

Race for a Miracle 124

*When Time Moved Ahead in
    Green Valley* 132

Chapter 4   **Testimonies of Prosperity** **139**

You Never Know Where a Dream

Might Lead 140

An Investment of the Heart 148

Award-Winning Faith 157

From Broken Dreams

to Beautiful Reality 164

The Bottom Line 171

The Sweet Smell of Success 178

With Long Life He Satisfies Them 186

Chapter 5   **Testimonies of Deliverance** **191**

Help Me, God! I'll Do Anything! 192

In the Ranks of a Royal Army 199

Now He Weeps for Joy 203

Free at Last 209

Climbing the Mountain 216

Introduction

Since the very first time we began publishing testimonies in the *Believer's Voice of Victory* magazine, I look forward to this part of each issue. I love to hear what God is doing in the lives of our Partners all over the world. These stories inspire and encourage me. What great stories of God's miraculous power and believers' undaunted faith in Him, and from the letters we have received over the years, reading them has encouraged your faith as well.

Time and time again we've received letters of how a Partner experienced an emergency situation or critical report, and the first thought they had was of a testimony article they had read in the *Believer's Voice of Victory.* They just knew if God did it once, He would do it again. That gave them the courage to stand for what God said, and not be moved by the circumstances. That testimony gave them the encouragement they needed to hang on, stay in faith and keep their mouth speaking God's Word.

As we live out the last days, and difficult situations occur, we need an awareness on the inside of us of God's power to heal, to deliver and to prosper. We need an awareness of the anointing to live every day in victory. We need to keep ourselves stirred up and the switch of faith turned on.

As you read these testimonies of faith, remember, they are people just like you who dared to step out on God's Word, who chose to speak faith and not unbelief, who were willing to believe God when others lost hope. They are real people, who had real needs, who experienced great victory. Allow their stories to minister to you the truth of God's love, His mercy, His provisions, and His willingness to heal. I know you'll be blessed.

—*Gloria Copeland*

CHAPTER 1

Testimonies of Faith

*"Now faith is the assurance
(the confirmation, the title-deed)
of the things [we] hope for, being the proof
of things [we] do not see and the conviction
of their reality—faith perceiving as real fact
what is not revealed to the senses."*

Hebrews 11:1, The Amplified Bible

Faith in Bloom

The Miraculous Birth of the Yellow African Violet

by Melanie Hemry

God had spoken. Nolan Blansit had never considered himself a spiritual giant—but he knew enough to recognize that voice.

Gripping the steering wheel, he fixed his gaze on the road ahead. A verdant host of leaves and stems and flowers bowed and waved at him from the roadside as he sped past. A serious student of plant genetics, Nolan had been awed by their variety and abundance during this trip across the Northwest. But now, he stared past them, his attention riveted on the astonishing words he'd just heard.

I want you to trust Me for the yellow African violet.

"The words came out of nowhere," Nolan recalls. "Although it wasn't an audible voice, the words were so clear and concise, I caught my breath."

A yellow African violet.

The thought of it hung, shimmering with inspiration, in Nolan's mind. African violet breeders had been reaching for that dream for 50 years. But research had proven such a violet was scientifically impossible to produce. The pigments in the existing strains contained no yellow at all.

Few others could have grasped the implications of God's words. But Nolan knew his wife Cindy would. He glanced at her, sitting beside him in the passenger seat, her Bible open on her lap.

"Cindy," he said, "the strangest thing just happened. God just told me to trust Him for a yellow African violet."

Her look of astonishment matched his own. So did the shock of her reply. "He just told me the same thing," she said.

"The next instant," Nolan recalls, "God impressed me to use Matthew 18:19 as the basis for my faith. But before I could tell Cindy, she had turned in her Bible to that exact passage."

"'If two of you shall agree on earth as touching any thing that they shall ask, it shall be done for them of my Father which is in heaven.' That verse," she announced, "will serve as the foundation for this miracle."

Just that summer, Nolan and Cindy had attended a meeting in Tulsa, Oklahoma, where they'd heard Kenneth Copeland for the first time. His teachings had ignited their faith and convinced them to trust God for His very best. But they'd never dreamed His "best" would include anything like this.

"We reached across the car seat," Nolan remembers and prayed. "Thank You, Father. We receive Your Word and trust You for this miracle." At that moment, they knew a yellow violet had just been born in the spirit realm.

Others, however, failed to share their faith. "When we got home and told friends we were going to have the first yellow African violet, people looked at us like we were crazy," says Nolan. "But I knew that Abram changed his name to Abraham—the father of many nations—years before Isaac was born."

Sure enough, two long years passed before Nolan was even able to begin work on the violets. "My faith hadn't wavered," he says, "but I had to face reality. God told me to believe Him for the yellow violet, but He didn't tell me *how* to breed it." Would the yellow come from genetic manipulation or from a seedling? Nolan had no idea.

Selecting hardy plants for breeding, Nolan chose not to use genetic manipulation techniques such as cell fusion. "I sensed there was only one way the yellow violet could be born—and that was as a gift from God."

For the next few years, Nolan did what every plant breeder had done for generations before him. He bred African violets. Then, in 1981, he crossed a blue and white violet with one that was pink and white. It was nothing unusual, really. He'd done it hundreds of times before. "But this time," Nolan remembers, "when the seedling flowered, there was the tiniest streak of yellow on the bloom."

What a day! "Nolan came bounding up the stairs with the flower," says Cindy. "We were so excited, we couldn't take our eyes off that bloom."

After that, Nolan began the tedious task of "selfing"— a process in which the plant is used to pollinate its own bloom. Then came the task of breeding yellow-gene violets with other hardy strains. *It won't be long now,* Nolan thought as yellow appeared on more and more seedlings.

But he was wrong. Instead of continuing to inch forward, Nolan suddenly found his project slipping back. As new generations of the plants were bred, the yellow began to disappear. In time, not one trace of yellow remained.

Depression settled over Nolan like a blanket. He spent days lying on the sofa without even speaking. The devil had used depression against him before, but he had always been able to get through it. This time, however, there seemed no way out.

Other things began to go wrong. One disappointment was piled on another. Finally, the Blansits' marriage crumbled under the strain. "The divorce papers were filed. Our home and possessions sold for only cents on the dollar," Nolan recalls. "Cindy was in Kentucky, and I threw away every seedling before leaving for Texas."

Months passed as Nolan and Cindy suffered their own private agonies. It seemed everything they'd worked for—and believed for—had come to an end. "The only thing needed to finalize it all was my signature on the divorce papers," says Nolan. "Then, suddenly, Cindy called me and said, 'Don't sign!'"

Abruptly, the couple reunited. Neither of them could see how the marriage could be put back together. But they had learned one thing from the yellow African violet—they could have *anything* they agreed on in prayer. They agreed on marriage.

"All those who saw Nolan Blansit's yellow African violet blossoms at the Kansas City [African Violet] Convention experienced spine-tingling chills followed by a sharp rise in temperature. This fever of excitement and expectation was brought about by the realization that their eyes were beholding perhaps the most amazing genetic advance in the history of violets. They were viewing the *impossible!*"

**AFRICAN VIOLET MAGAZINE,
September/October 1989**

The couple thought sadly of all they'd thrown away. A house, furniture...the seedlings that had taken so many years to produce. But they did have one thing left. Determined to save a few precious fragments of hope—for their marriage and for their miracle—Cindy had carefully sealed away a few African violet seed pods in an envelope. Those seeds gave them their new start.

Nolan sowed the seeds and tended them much the way he and Cindy were now tending and cultivating their marriage. "I kept thinking about one of Brother Copeland's messages on forgiveness," Nolan says. "I couldn't see it all then, but I knew that as Cindy and I let go of the unforgiveness between us, the Spirit was freed to move in our lives."

Within a matter of months, seven seedlings bloomed with yellow markings. The year was 1983. A full six years had passed since God had asked them to trust Him for the yellow violet.

Nolan, working full time in landscape design, came home every evening and nurtured along the breeding process. Slowly, the yellow color began to spread.

In 1989, Nolan and Cindy finally held the miracle of the yellow African violet tenderly in their hands. God had kept His promise. Although He had required them to tend it with faith and patience, He was the One Who had planted it in their hearts. And, in the end, He was the One Who had made it bloom.

Two weeks before the National African Violet Society of America held their convention, *African Violet Magazine* sported a picture of the Blansits' yellow African violet on the cover. At the convention in Kansas City, people from Japan, Australia, South Africa and South America crowded around for a glimpse of the famous flower and for autographs from the Blansits.

Later, in the meeting hall, as Nolan Blansit stood at the podium, the group waited in anticipation. Their unspoken question rang silently through the room. How had he done the impossible? How had he bred the yellow African violet?

"It was a gift from God," Nolan said simply.

Few there would ever fully understand the implications of his words. They'd never know the difference that gift had made in the Blansits' lives. Nor would they ever realize how desperately the devil fought it.

Why would God choose to give such a peculiar gift? And why would Satan fear it so? The Blansits themselves have asked those questions often. Even now the answer isn't entirely clear. But there are clues. The name Cindy and Nolan chose for it, for instance—His Golden Glory. And the fact that the Blansits committed to spending the income received when the flowers sold to the public in 1992 to spreading the gospel.

When asked what is next, the sparkle in Nolan's eyes reveals that for him this miracle is not over yet. He described the shades that have already blossomed as a result of His Golden Glory. Orange, peach, salmon, yellow and white..."It's even possible to have a pure red African violet now! I have seven seedlings with the faintest trace of red," Nolan says, barely able to contain his excitement.

What will the Blansits name a pure red African violet? His Precious Blood, of course.

Nolan and Cindy have been Partners with Kenneth Copeland Ministries for 17 years!

From Hart to Hearts

by Melanie Hemry

Johnny Hart stepped outside his home in rural New York for the short walk to his studio. Inhaling the pungent aroma of woodlands and wildflowers, he gazed appreciatively across the beautiful 150 acres that was now his own.

Some days he still had trouble believing how far his dream had taken him. He'd been like most kids growing up—in love with cartoons. The only difference between Johnny Hart and most of the world was that he never lost that love.

Johnny remembered the high school counselor who'd asked him what he wanted to do with his life. His answer had been instant and honest. Draw. He never considered doing anything else. The dream that seemed so simple to him as a child had ultimately been anything but simple to attain. Yet he'd never given up—even though at times it had seemed as illusive as the white strands of cloud now floating above him in the blue New York sky.

Stepping off the porch, Johnny shook off the memories of those hard years. Now, in 1987, they were far behind him. His first cartoon strip, *B.C.,* had become a syndicated success in 1958. Four years later he had created a second cartoon strip, *The Wizard of Id.*

For years now Johnny had drawn to his heart's content, basking in the success of both cartoons. By the world's standard Johnny Hart had it all—the career of his dreams, a solid marriage to his wife, Bobby, two daughters, Patti and Perri, grandchildren...financial security.

Why then, Johnny wondered as he settled into his studio that morning, *do I still feel a void in my life, like something is missing?* What else could one man possibly want? In days past, when the questions had become too pressing and the aching void too uncomfortable, Johnny had at times numbed the pain with alcohol.

But no more. Today Johnny Hart determined that he was going to fill that emptiness. And he had a strong suspicion that what he would need to do it was the one thing he didn't have in his life right now—a relationship with God.

"I went to a Methodist Sunday school when I was growing up," Johnny remembers. "As an adult, I was a good, moral, upright person. The kind of person the world figures can earn his way into heaven. Of course, the only person with that right was Jesus Christ, but I'd pushed Him aside in 1964 when my mother died of cancer. I guess I got mad at God over her death and went on about my life without giving Him the honor and worship He deserves."

Although Johnny didn't realize it on that morning six years ago, the fact was that even though he had turned his back on God, God had never given up on *him.* No doubt, He had even been involved in bringing the Hart family to their new home on this rustic 150-acre site.

"Bobby and I were very comfortable living in Endicott, New York," Johnny explains, "when a real estate agent asked us to look at some property in a small town nearby. We bought the property, and after we moved we had to get a satellite dish to get good television reception. Suddenly, I had more TV programs to choose from than I ever had before."

As Johnny explored those programs, the ones he found himself choosing most consistently were those with a strong Christian message. One of them was *Believer's Voice of Victory.*

"I started watching Kenneth Copeland because he was so funny," Johnny says. "He was better than most comedians I'd seen. While I was laughing, his message of truth hit me between the eyes.

"All my life I'd heard about the importance of faith in God. But I'd never heard anyone teach exactly what faith was until I heard Kenneth and Gloria."

One of the faith principles that stirred Johnny most was the power of faith-filled words. Ironically, his life had been one long example that such words work—with or without conscious assent.

"When I was a young man in the Air Force," Johnny recalls, "I came home from work every night and sat at a card table to draw. I still remember the frustration of having a clear mental image of what I wanted to draw, yet being unable to duplicate it on paper.

"One night I'd tried for hours to put an image on paper. I was so tired I accidentally spilled ink over all my work. I snapped, kicking over the card table and everything on it. I shouted my frustration, ranting like a madman."

Johnny looked up and saw his wife, Bobby, standing in the doorway. "Before I'm 27 years old," he shouted, "I *will* have a nationally syndicated comic strip!"

Later, Johnny felt embarrassed at his outburst. But his words hadn't been the spouting of an over-inflated ego. He'd spoken out of the deep conviction of his heart. Why he shouted 27 remains a mystery.

"After my discharge from the Air Force I worked night and day trying to sell cartoons to national magazines,"

Johnny explains. "I succeeded in selling to magazines like the *Saturday Evening Post*. But the income wasn't steady enough to support a family. Finally, I gave up and went to work in the art department at General Electric."

Even then, however, Johnny didn't stop drawing cartoons. Night after night he worked at developing his own style. He'd already discovered that his style ran to cave men. For years Johnny submitted cave men cartoons to magazine editors who sent them back with a polite note.

One day at work Johnny surprised himself by announcing, "Tonight I'm going home and create a nationally famous comic strip!"

That night, Johnny Hart created the cave man comic strip, *B.C.*

"Bobby suggested I base the characters on real people," Johnny recalls. "Peter and Thor were based on two men I worked with. My best friend became Clumsy Carp. My brother-in-law, Wiley, is a fastidious man who lost a leg in World War II. I made him a slovenly fellow with a wooden leg in my cartoon."

Johnny completed 24 strips and submitted them to a syndicate. They were rejected. He sent them to another syndicate. Rejected again. Almost a year after he'd created *B.C.* Johnny still hadn't come any closer to selling the strip.

"I submitted *B.C.* to the Associated Press syndicate," Johnny remembers, "and I hadn't heard anything back from them. Finally, I went to New York City and presented myself to the editor. He didn't remember my work. He searched his desk and emptied every drawer.

"He found *B.C.* on the bottom of the last drawer. On top of *B.C.* was another strip he hadn't bought by one of my favorite cartoonists. He waved it at me.

"Now *here's a good* cartoon," he said. "Nobody buys cave men. You need to find another angle and start over. Besides, we don't even buy comic strips."

Johnny felt like somebody had died. He stood outside the Rockefeller Center and tried to come to terms with his failure. The editor's words replayed in his mind like a broken record. *Nobody buys cave men.*

"I took the envelope filled with my work and walked over to a trash container labeled, 'Keep New York City Clean.' I was about to drop the envelope into the trash when another thought flashed through my mind. *Besides we don't buy comic strips.*

"That editor doesn't even *buy* comics! How could he be such an authority on my work? I found a directory of newspaper syndicates and walked to those nearby. I didn't sell my cartoons that day, but I left New York City with the conviction that I wouldn't give up."

Back home, Johnny mailed *B.C.* to the *New York Herald Tribune* syndicate.

They bought it.

B.C. first appeared in newspapers nationally February 17, 1958. That evening Bobby asked Johnny if he remembered what he'd said the night he kicked over the card table.

"No," Johnny said, reflecting on that night, "but whatever it was, I'm sure it doesn't bear repeating."

"You said you'd have a nationally syndicated comic strip before your 27th birthday."

The next day, February 18, 1958, was Johnny's birthday. His *27th* birthday.

Back then, Johnny Hart thought that was a strange coincidence. But in actuality, he had set a spiritual law in motion. A law found in Mark 11:23, *"Truly, I tell you, whosoever says to this mountain, Be lifted up and thrown into the sea! and does not doubt at all in his heart, but believes that what he says will take place, it will be done for him" (The Amplified Bible).*

Johnny Hart still uses that principle of faith-filled words today. But there's one big difference. Now he does it on purpose. He does it because he has a relationship with the God Who established the principle.

That relationship has been growing steadily ever since those days six years ago when he and Bobby began to watch the Copelands and other ministries via their new satellite dish. And, just as Johnny suspected it would, it has filled the once-empty place within them with a supernatural peace and joy.

You might even say it has filled them to overflowing for, although they still consider themselves "babes" in the Lord, they can be found every Sunday at their local church pouring out their hearts to a

> **"Before I'm 27 years old," Johnny shouted, "I will have a nationally syndicated comic strip!"**

Sunday school class full of teenagers, teaching them the principles of faith they themselves just began learning a few years ago.

Of course, throughout the week Johnny Hart still spends his time sketching cartoons. But these days, he often uses his characters to deliver more than a punch line. Especially on Christmas and Easter, he uses the voice God gave him through *B.C.* and *The Wizard of Id* to *"Go into all the world and...publish openly the good news..."* (Mark 16:15, *The Amplified Bible*).

Although Johnny never sees most of the people who hear his message, he knows by the letters he receives that they are out there listening.

"Most of my mail is positive," Johnny says, "although

there are always dissenters. Some people try to make me a hero for speaking up through a newspaper syndicate, but I don't see it that way. Too many Christians have bought into the lie that we shouldn't mention our beliefs. It's almost like, as Christians, we don't have rights. That's not true. We have every right, *and* the Great Commission."

For Christmas, 1992, Johnny drew Thor and Peter walking in the shadow of the North Star.

"That star made a shadow," one of them says.

"Don't be ridiculous," the other retorts. "The only way it can do that is if something brighter than the star is behind the star!"

"Like what?"

"A sun, maybe."

"A SON?..."

There is no question that Someone brighter than the sun shines behind Johnny Hart and his cartoon friends. And through them, that Someone is sending smiles and glimpses of the good news from Hart to hearts around the world.

Johnny and Bobby have been Partners with Kenneth Copeland Ministries for 10 years!

The Final Decree

by Melanie Hemry

*D*IVORCE. The judge slammed the stamp onto each paper in rapid succession. Judy Myers gripped the counter, feeling each stamp imprinted on her heart—castaway...rejected...worthless....

Steven stood casually beside her. Steven, her husband of ten years. Steven, the tall, burly hero who always made her feel so beautiful. Steven, the father of her children. Steven, who had left her for another woman. Steven, who had asked these people to stamp these papers and cut her out of his life.

Judy stumbled out of the courthouse and sank onto a nearby bench. Divorced. So final. Cradling her head in her hands, Judy remembered when divorce had been an unthinkable word in their marriage.

Then she had met Jesus and for some reason things began to change. Judy remembered running home to tell Steven about Him. They told each other everything in those days. Steven looked at her in an odd sort of way and said, "That's nice."

That's nice? The more she told Steven about her relationship with the Lord, the more distant he became. Until finally, 2¹/₂ years ago, he'd moved out—into the arms of another woman.

During the pain-ridden days after Steven left, Judy first heard Kenneth Copeland teach on being redeemed from the curse of the law. She had hurried to her Bible and looked it up for herself. Sure enough, Deuteronomy 28:30 listed one of the curses under the law, *"Thou shalt betroth a wife, and another man shall lie with her...".* Wife or husband, infidelity was all a part of the same curse.

Then she flipped the pages of her Bible over to Galatians 3:13: *"Christ hath redeemed us from the curse of the law, being made a curse for us: for it is written, Cursed is every one that hangeth on a tree...."*

Judy's heart leaped within her. Christ had redeemed her from a broken marriage! She decided there and then to believe the Word and not her circumstances.

Three times in the 2¹/₂ years since he'd first moved out, Steven had returned home. But even then, though they lived under the same roof, he and Judy remained poles apart. He never gave up the other woman, and Judy never gave up the Word. They had nowhere to compromise.

"Steven went for weeks without even talking to the children," Judy remembers. "The Lord gave me Mark 11:23-24 to stand on, about speaking to the mountain to be removed and be cast into the sea. Then He showed me verses 25-26, *'And when ye stand praying, forgive, if ye have aught against any: that your Father also which is in heaven may forgive you your trespasses. But if ye do not forgive, neither will your Father which is in heaven forgive your trespasses.'"*

Judy had a lot to forgive and she knew it wouldn't be easy. But she had to do it. Her entire stand of faith hinged on her willingness to forgive—not just Steven, but the other woman as well.

"It was tough," Judy recalls. "She would call and harass me, saying that Steven didn't love me and that I was a bad wife to him. The Lord kept reminding me of 1 Corinthians 13:8, *'Love never fails...'* *(The Amplified Bible).*

"Finally, I talked her into meeting me in person.

When she stepped out of her car, I just walked over and put my arms around her. I explained that I didn't have anything against her, but I knew Steven would come back to me. I couldn't afford to be bitter and I had to walk in love."

Sitting now outside the courthouse, Judy wondered what she should do. Despite 2½ years of prayers and forgiveness and her faith that their marriage would be restored, Steven had divorced her. Should she give up that faith now? Was the divorce court's pronouncement the final decree?

That night, Judy turned her Bible to the now familiar passage in Malachi 2:14:

> Yet you ask, Why does He reject it? Because the Lord was witness [to the covenant made at your marriage] between you and the wife of your youth, against whom you have dealt treacherously and to whom you were faithless. Yet she is your companion and the wife of your covenant... *(The Amplified Bible).*

Judy rolled the last few words of that passage over and over again in her mind. *"Yet she is your companion and the wife of your covenant."* Divorced or not, Judy knew God still recognized her as Steven's wife.

"I realized God would not override a person's will or manipulate them," Judy explains, "so I was careful not to pray that way. I prayed against the god of this world who had blinded Steven's eyes. I asked the Father to speak to his heart." It would be years before Judy knew specifically how those prayers were answered.

In the meantime, one of the most difficult things for Judy was watching their children, Kirstin and Kyle, suffer from the lack of their father's attention. She began to pray Malachi 4:6 over the situation, *"And he will restore the hearts of the fathers to their children, and the hearts of the children to their fathers, lest I come and smite the land with a curse" (New American Standard).*

The hardest day for Judy in each passing year was their anniversary—Valentine's Day. Steven had always gotten her wonderful cards, and each year he'd told her that their marriage was so special the whole world celebrated with them. Now she spent those once-precious Valentine's Days alone.

In May 1981, four years after Steven moved out, he phoned with the news she'd prayed for so long. "Hi," he said, "I got saved last night."

He spoke the words matter-of-factly. There was no fanfare. No fireworks. But Judy knew those words would eventually change everything.

Once Steven accepted the Lord, the relationship he was in didn't work anymore. Soon, he moved out of the woman's house and into his own apartment. Gradually, he began spending more time with Judy and the children, but he made it clear that he still maintained his friendship with the other woman.

"I wanted to challenge him on his relationship with her," Judy admits, "but the Lord reminded me that He allows the wheat and tares to grow together until it's time for Him to separate them."

By now, Judy had become a Christian writer and spent many hours a day studying the Word. She was growing rapidly in the Lord. "I wanted Steven to be the spiritual leader," she explains. "So I prayed, telling the Lord that I didn't want to be the head of our household. Afterward, every time I saw Steven he had grasped some new revelation that it had taken me years to learn. His growth in the Lord was fast and solid."

Before long, Steven began attending church with Judy and their children. He developed the habit of staying over for Sunday lunch and spending the afternoon with them. Sunday night they each drove their own car to church. Afterward, Steven always kissed Judy goodnight before sending her home.

As weeks stretched into months, Judy fought impatience. *When is the breakthrough going to come?* she wondered. Then one afternoon as Judy listened to Kenneth Copeland tapes and painted her garage, she heard the answer. Without warning, the Holy Spirit spoke four words that took her breath away: *It's not many days.*

"I constantly had to resist the urge to take things into my own hands," Judy admits. "So instead of getting excited and overeager, I told myself that with God a day is as a thousand years. I turned off my emotions and simply painted the garage."

Eight days later, Steven phoned. He wanted to see Judy—alone. When he arrived, he was choked with emotion. "Judy," he said, "I've been such a jerk."

"God has forgiven you, and I've forgiven you," Judy answered.

Finally, as though from a far distance, Judy heard the words she'd waited four long years to hear. "I love you, and I'd like to spend the rest of my life with you."

"I had to be careful," Judy explains. "I knew that love wasn't enough. Steven had to know it was God's will for me to be his wife. I had to be certain that during the next storm he'd stand on the Word instead of his emotions."

"Besides love," Judy asked, "why else?"

"You're a wonderful mother," Steven said.

"Why else?"

"Well, I wasn't going to say this, because it isn't romantic, but...I spent the weekend in a tent praying and listening to God, and I know it's His will for you to be my wife."

"Yes!" Judy screamed and tumbled into his lap.

On October 23, 1982, Steven and Judy were remarried.

"The Lord healed our marriage," Judy says, "but there was one detail that still bothered me. I felt cheated out of our special anniversary date. When I prayed about it, the Lord reminded me of Joel 2:25, *'And I will restore to you the years that the locust hath eaten, the cankerworm, and the caterpillar, and the palmerworm....'"*

A few years later, on Valentine's Day—their original anniversary—Steven handed Judy a card. When she opened it, her gaze fell to the words he'd written there. Reading them she felt as though warm oil was pouring over her, healing every emotional scar that remained from the separation and divorce. The card simply said, "On this day in 1970 God gave me His best."

Today, the Myers celebrate their anniversary once again on a day so special the whole world celebrates with them. Both Steven and Judy are active in their church. Judy, Kirstin and Kyle all teach Sunday school. Steven teaches a Bible study, is a deacon, and both Steven and Judy are Care Team Leaders in their church.

What does Judy have to say now to others who are navigating rough marital waters? "If you want to weather the storms of life without being completely destroyed, you must build your life on the Word of God. I learned that early from Brother Copeland.

"He was teaching from Luke 6:46-49, where Jesus told the story about the person who hears and obeys the Word. Jesus said that person is like a man who, building a house, dug deep and laid his foundation on a rock. When the flood arose and the torrent broke against his house, it could not be destroyed because of its secure foundation.

"But the person who merely hears the Word and does not put it into practice is like the man who built his house on the sand. When the storm arose against *his* house, it collapsed immediately.

"I didn't know the Word when the storm struck my marriage. Our relationship wasn't based on godly principles, but on infatuation, so when I started basing my role of wife on the Word it was like building a house during a hurricane.

Sitting now outside the courthouse, Judy wondered what she should do. Despite 2½ years of prayers and forgiveness and her faith that their marriage would be restored, Steven had divorced her.

"Still, I laid hold of Jesus' promise and believed the storm could not prevail if I acted on the Word. Jesus said, '...*In the world you have tribulation...but...take courage...for I have overcome the world.—I have deprived it of power to harm, have conquered it [for you]*' (John 16:33, *The Amplified Bible).* It's not easy to build a house while the wind is blowing and floodwaters are rising, but it's possible through faith in God's Word.

"The Word works. It is the Manufacturer's Handbook containing prescribed repair and preventative maintenance for successful living. It will work for whoever puts it to work."

It certainly worked for the Myers. In their lives it proved to be powerful enough to overturn divorce. In their lives the Word became the final decree.

Editor's Note: To protect the confidences of friends and family, the names have been changed in this article.

Update: It's been 13 years since Judy and Steven were restored...and they say it just keeps getting better and better!

Steven and Judy have been Partners with Kenneth Copeland Ministries for 17 years!

CHAPTER 2

Testimonies of Protection

*"For he shall give his angels
charge over thee, to keep thee in all thy ways.
They shall bear thee up in their hands, lest
thou dash thy foot against a stone."*

Psalm 91:11-12

A Path Through Mighty Waters

by Melanie Hemry

Tuesday, November 12, 1991. Del Hicks gazed out the window of the plane at the blue skies of the Bahamas. Glancing down at his watch, he quickly figured that if things went as scheduled, this charter flight would have him in Fort Lauderdale by supper time.

As a boat captain who frequently sailed the waters off the Florida east coast, Del had made this trip home many times. But today was different.

Today he wasn't just heading back to see his wife and children. He was going to attend the funeral of a good friend. A wave of sadness washed over Del's heart. Resting his head heavily against the seat back, he listened to the droning of the engines and began to doze.

Suddenly, Del jerked his eyes open. Something about the Piper Seneca's engines didn't sound right. Leaning forward, he looked over the pilot's shoulder at the radar screen. They were about 25 miles from the island of Bimini and 50 miles east of Fort Lauderdale.

Del listened again. The sputter and silence told him all he needed to know. The twin-engine plane had just lost one engine.

Seconds later, the pilot's voice sliced through the tense stillness. "Open the door and lighten the load!" Jumping from his seat, Del shoved open the exit door against the rushing wind and began to heave luggage into the emptiness outside.

But it didn't help. The second engine began to sputter...then stopped.

The tiny aircraft fell at a dizzy pace toward the steely stretch of ocean below. Yet, oddly enough, instead of colliding violently with it, the airplane glided across the water as though supported by angel's wings.

The five people aboard knew there was no time to waste. As the plane began to sink, they scrambled for the door. Del, who was closest to the door went first, followed by *Frank and Ann Powell, the couple who had chartered the flight. Passenger Dan Tuckfield and the pilot were close behind. One by one they slid down the wing and splashed into the chilly waters of the Atlantic.

Only a few minutes of floundering in the relentless waves convinced most of the group that the best course of action would be to swim immediately toward Bimini. But Del disagreed. "We'd crashed in the Flats," Del explains. "There's a strong current that flows from there to the Gulf Stream. With the tide out, I knew that current would sweep us away and we'd never make it to Bimini."

Finally they agreed to stay put until the tide came in—but how?

The pilot remembered a 10-foot canvas tarp stashed in the airplane. If they could get to it, they might be able to use it to secure themselves somehow. But the plane was resting on the bottom below them.

Then Dan Tuckfield had an idea. The youngest of the group, 35-year-old Dan, was an expert swimmer. Diving 15-20 feet down to the wreckage, he retrieved the canvas, life vests for them all, his wet suit, fins and mask. Strangely, it was the only time he had taken his swimming gear onto an airplane with him. No one knew just how crucial that gear would prove to be.

Attaching a line to each end of the tarp, Dan dove back down to the wreckage and tied one end to the tail of the plane. The survivors tied themselves to the other end of the line and let the airplane anchor them against the tide. For four hours the rope and canvas held them while the tide tried to tug them into the Gulf Stream.

"About 9 that evening the tide changed," Del recalls. "By then we knew the emergency signal must not have worked, because there hadn't been any planes overhead searching for us. It was dark, and we could see the beacon light from Bimini in the distance. We figured the best thing to do was start swimming toward that light."

Easier said than done. Since Mrs. Powell couldn't swim at all, one of the other four had to constantly hold her. That, along with the cold water and the 2-foot waves, slowed the swimmers to a crawl.

"After two hours we hadn't made any real progress. So we tied ourselves together in a huddle and just treaded water."

Shivering and exhausted, Del remembered the teaching he and his wife, Pat, had heard from Gloria Copeland on the 91st Psalm. They had taken that teaching seriously. Now, adrift in the ocean and struggling to stay alive, Del knew why. Softly, he began reciting the words he'd said every day for months now. "He who dwells in the secret place of the Most High shall abide under the shadow of the Almighty...."

Pat Hicks paced the waiting area inside customs at a private airport in Ft. Lauderdale. She talked with her daughter, Alicia, and joked with her grandchildren,

Latitia and Amber. Occasionally she searched the sky for a glimpse of the plane that would bring her husband, Del, home.

Del. She could hardly wait to see him. The death of their good friend, Gene Caswell, following just months after the death of another good friend, Bob Salmi, had cast a shadow over her that could only be brightened by Del's smiling eyes and the words he always said when he stepped through customs. "Hey, Baby...."

Hour after hour passed as Pat paced and scanned the horizon. Still, no plane. No Del. As darkness began to creep over the Atlantic, Pat stared at her daughter Alicia, and asked the question no one had dared voice. "Where is your Daddy?"

By 6 o'clock that evening the Coast Guard had launched the largest search and rescue mission in Florida's history.

Hey baby...hey baby...hey baby, the devil mocked. *You'll never hear those words again!*

"I found a nook in the wall," Pat remembers, "and buried my face in it. I told God that if Paul and Silas could praise Him in their circumstances, I could too. It was a sacrifice to praise. I told the Lord, 'I don't know where Del is, but I know he lives in the 91st Psalm. I know You are our God, and wherever he is right now, You are his refuge.'"

Pat and Alicia were quiet during the drive from Ft. Lauderdale to their home in Miami. Then the Lord spoke to Pat. *Read Isaiah 43.* Turning on the map light, she read these words, *"Thus says the Lord, Who makes a way through the sea And a path through the mighty waters...."*

"My house was full when we got home," Pat recalls. "Our son, Del II, was waiting, along with our son-in-law

Herbie, our pastors, Brad and Lynette Flook, and other friends and family.

"We gathered together and prayed for Del's safety and continued protection. We surrounded him with warring angels. I asked that wherever Del was, he'd never be afraid, hungry or thirsty. Once we prayed, we continued to praise God for His faithfulness."

Pat didn't even try to sleep. Every time she closed her eyes, the devil replayed scenes of fiery airplane crashes in her mind. Finally she lay down to rest. *Don't you know Del's dead?* the devil whispered. *Bob's dead. Gene's dead. Death always comes in threes!*

"No!" Pat answered fiercely. "I'm in covenant with Almighty God! I will not be afraid of the terror by night!" Then she stood her ground, praying in the Spirit and speaking God's promises until morning.

Wednesday, November 13, 1991. The first rays of the sun spilled over the horizon bringing warmth to Del and his four companions as they bobbed helplessly in the salty waves. Del's right leg cramped so badly he couldn't use it anymore. His arms ached with the effort of holding Mrs. Powell.

Throughout the night, Mr. Powell had called everyone's name to keep them awake. But now, except for the rhythmic swish of the waves, all went silent as Frank Powell gave up his heroic struggle for life and died.

"Mrs. Powell didn't have much strength left either," Del says, remembering that sad morning. "We tied her to us, resting her legs across Dan's shoulders. I held her chest and head out of the water. Danny also held onto Mr. Powell's body in the hope that we could get him home for burial."

But that afternoon, death approached again in another form—a tiger shark, the third most dangerous shark in the ocean. "I'm scared of tiger sharks," Del admits, "and that shark—all 10 feet of him—was eyeball to eyeball with me. Yet fear didn't touch me. I knew I was protected."

When it became clear the shark was about to attack, the group agreed to release Mr. Powell's body as a distraction. Sure enough, the shark disappeared.

They continued to tread water. *So tired.* Del couldn't remember ever being so tired and cold. Hours passed. Then the drone of an engine brought Del instantly alert. A helicopter! He watched it approach, growing larger and larger.

Hearts pounding, the four remaining survivors waved their arms at the helicopter. It passed by. Was it circling? No. It continued on, becoming a distant speck on the horizon...then disappeared.

"Late that afternoon, Mrs. Powell died. Her heart was broken, her hope gone," Del remembers. "With every hour that passed, things looked more bleak. But instead of giving up, I praised God—sometimes under my breath, most of the time out loud. That's all I could do, just speak His praises."

Pat watched the sun rise Wednesday morning with joy. Surely today the searchers would find Del and bring him home. With three Coast Guard stations, 16 private planes (two of which were owned by Del's employer, Charles Krasne) and who knows how many boats involved in the search, how could they fail?

But the day dragged on with no sighting. "I pulled out my teaching tape by Gloria Copeland on the 91st Psalm," Pat says. "I put it on the stereo and played it all day. When it stopped, I just turned it over and played it again."

That afternoon, a reporter from a local news station arrived at the Hicks' home. The reporter questioned Pat. "How are you maintaining your composure? You don't show any hysteria."

"It's called the peace of God," Pat explained to the world.

Del tried to remember what it felt like to be warm. He tried to recall the merciless afternoon sun on Chub Cay, but he couldn't. His body, bruised from the hours of holding Mrs. Powell, felt every one of his 58 years. When he was too cold to move, he lost consciousness.

Dan Tuckfield knew their only chance now was for him to make it to Cat Cay. Wearing his wet suit and fins, he left Del and the pilot and began to swim. He kept on all night—mile after mile. And at dawn Thursday morning, he stumbled onto the shore. Calling for help, he was taken to customs where he notified the Coast Guard of the two survivors' location.

At 9 o'clock that morning the Coast Guard spotted what appeared to be a corpse, buoyed by a yellow life vest, drifting in the ocean. But it was no corpse. It was Captain Del Hicks—and he was alive.

Rescue workers were unable to bend his frozen legs to put him in the basket and lift him from the water. So they simply laid him across it. Strangely, they noted, there were no sharks in sight.

An hour later the pilot was also rescued alive— encircled by sharks!

Thursday, November 14, 1991. At 6 o'clock in the morning, Pat Hicks woke with pure peace and excitement. Waking everybody in the house, she said, "Worship God! It's over! Can't you feel it? It's over!"

Dressing carefully, she put on Del's favorite perfume. Then she waited for the call. And, just as she expected, it came.

Del Hicks was admitted to Jackson Memorial Hospital with a body temperature of 83 degrees. Doctors placed him on the heart-lung machine and circulated his blood through a warmer. Afterward, in intensive care, Pat hovered over his bed waiting for him to wake up and talk to her. All that day and night she waited. Friday morning she went home to change clothes. Calling back to the hospital she asked the nurse how her husband was doing.

"Just a moment," the nurse said. Minutes later, Pat heard a familiar voice say two words:

"Hey, Baby...."

In that split second of overwhelming joy, Pat Hicks praised the God of the 91st Psalm. The God Who had kept His promises and made *a way through the sea, a path through the mighty waters.* The God Who had brought her husband safely home.

The five people aboard knew there was no time to waste. As the plane began to sink, they scrambled for the door. One by one they slid down the wing and splashed into the chilly waters of the Atlantic.

*Editor's Note: As a courtesy to their family members, the names of the deceased couple have been changed.

Update: Two weeks after Del's blood was removed, warmed, and recirculated, a two-foot long blood clot formed in his leg. As his leg swelled double its normal size, Del and Pat stood on Psalm 118:17 claiming Del's life. Doctors were uncertain whether he would live or die.

Del survived, but the doctors said the clot would probably remain, and pose a threat at any time. Two years later, in 1994, Del became ill. Both the Hicks and their doctor were concerned that the clot was the problem. Completion of tests revealed the clot was gone.

The "dissolved blood clot story" has become the conclusion of the Hicks' testimony of God's faithfulness and protection.

Dell and Pat have been Partners with Kenneth Copeland Ministries for 9 years!

Code Name: PRAYER

by Melanie Hemry

April 5, 1993.

Capt. Steve Toller arrived early at McGuire Air Force Base. Walking briskly through the passenger terminal, he mentally reviewed the details of the assignment ahead.

In just a few hours, he and his men—an elite group from the Explosive Ordnance Disposal (EOD) of the U.S. Army—would board a plane bound for Mogadishu, Somalia. Once there, the EOD's job would be simple and straightforward: Keep supply routes open so food can get through.

No one expected any problems, really. As always, there was an element of risk. But risk was something Toller's unit was accustomed to facing. Trained in handling bombs, explosives, and chemical, biological and nuclear weapons, the EOD was usually deployed when land mines, grenades and artillery shells were discovered unexploded. They worked with the Secret Service protecting the president and other dignitaries, and occasionally responded to calls from the police departments. Those were routine assignments. This one, however, was not.

According to the briefings Steve had received, there was no need for great concern. The situation was tense, but under control. Those in the know predicted that things would continue to improve slowly, until the U.S. military presence would no longer be needed.

As his men boarded the plane, Steve watched wives and children grab last hugs and kisses. He'd never had to tell the wife of one of his men that she was a widow. He shook his head to dismiss the thought. After all, they weren't going to war.

Still, Capt. Toller had been in the military for 17 years. During that time, he'd learned one valuable lesson: expect the unexpected.

After all goodbyes had been said, Steve called his men together. He glanced from face to face. They were a rugged group—used to walking on the edge of danger. He admired each of them.

"Most of you know," Steve began, "that my parents are ministers in Las Vegas. My dad gave me some scriptures and asked that I pray them as a prayer of protection over you."

Steve opened a Bible and turned to Isaiah 54:17, "In the words of the prophet Isaiah, I pray that, *'No weapon that is formed against [you] shall prosper.'"*

Turning to Psalm 91, Steve began to read, *"He that dwelleth in the secret place of the most High shall abide under the shadow of the Almighty...."*

"I'd like to seal our protection by taking communion. I don't have bread or wine, so these will have to do," Steve said, opening a pouch of anti-malaria pills. Handing each man his medication, Steve bowed his head. "Let us pray...."

Ambushed!

The first two months in Mogadishu passed slowly. As planned, Steve and his men worked steadily clearing routes for food transport. The U.S. Marines kept a tight security force and the warm, arid days passed uneventfully. Even so, Steve Toller continued to pray for his unit every day, and again before each mission.

On June 5, 1993, those prayers paid off.

That day, the men of the EOD had been dispatched to 21 October Road, not far from the site where confiscated weapons were being stored. Steve knew the United Nations had scheduled an inspection of the site. But two other such inspections had already taken place—each without incident. There seemed no reason to expect anything different this time.

But, unknown to Steve, this time was going to be different. This time there would be a massacre. For during the past few weeks, Somali warlord Gen. Mohammed Farah Hasan Aideed had been secretly stealing weapons from the storage sites. And today those weapons were turned on U.N. troops.

By day's end, 23 Pakistani soldiers had been brutally murdered and many others wounded. Steve's men, a scant quarter mile from the site of the ambush, returned fire. Back in their quarters, the men were shaken, but unharmed.

"Once Aideed's men were more heavily armed, the situation deteriorated rapidly," Steve recalls. "There were nighttime attacks at the university barracks, vehicles exploded along the road, and sniper fire increased.

"The EOD was ordered to destroy all the remaining ammunition storage sites before those weapons got into the hands of the warring factions. This time we knew there would be a fight. Aideed's men expected our move and we took fire. We had air cover from U.S. Cobra attack helicopters and an AC130 Spectre gunship. Resistance was encountered, but we destroyed 22 tons of weapons and munitions."

A few days later, the Pakistani infantry reported a roadblock and asked the EOD to check for booby traps. Steve and his men stopped their vehicle down the road and approached cautiously. Sometimes the blockades were rigged with bombs. Other times, snipers waited to ambush the troops who tried to reopen the road.

Capt. Toller scanned the landscape. It was quiet. Too quiet. He could feel the hair raise at the back of his neck. *Snipers.* He sensed their presence as surely as the mosquitoes that buzzed incessantly around him. Mosquitoes and snipers had a lot in common. They both wanted blood—his blood, and the blood of his men. Steve's goal was to thwart their mission.

Swatting a huge mosquito off his arm, Steve bowed his head for what seemed like the 1,000th time to pray.

He and his team crept forward. Just as he suspected, there was no bomb. This was the work of snipers. Rocks and abandoned vehicles blocked the road. They moved quickly, their own breathing seemed loud as they listened for the familiar sound of gunfire. Nothing. *Can't they see us?* Steve wondered. *Did God blind them to our presence?*

When the rocks were cleared, Steve and his men pushed the vehicles off the road. Back in their own vehicles, they sped away.

Minutes later, a U.S. truck drove past the spot. Gunfire and grenades exploded. The ambush was over in seconds.

Toller and his men heard the shots and stared at one another, stunned. *How? Why?* A thousand questions rushed through their minds. Steve recalled the words of Psalm 91, *"He that dwelleth in the secret place of the most High shall abide under the shadow of the Almighty"* (verse 1).

Day after day, on one mission after another, Steve saw those words at work. "There were many times when we arrived at the scene of unexploded mines and grenades," he says. "As we moved close to defuse the ordnance or blow it in place, sniper fire exploded around us. Bullets screamed past us. Yet, somehow, not one of the bullets found its mark against us."

Even unseen enemies like hepatitis, intestinal parasites and different strains of malaria which ran rampant among most troops in Somalia, failed to successfully attack the EOD. They seemed virtually immune to sickness and disease.

The Invasion

Within days of the first strike by Gen. Aideed, Steve received orders to assist a U.N. offensive of multinational troops in an invasion of Aideed's estate.

The palatial estate had become the headquarters of the warlord's operation. He and his top aides lived inside the compound, surrounded by massive, heavily guarded walls.

"The invasion was to take place on June 17," says Steve. "On June 16, we moved to the quarters of the Pakistani engineers which was close to Aideed's compound. Soldiers aren't too religious—until they get into a tight spot. That night, every man knew we were walking into a very tight spot. We listened to the Muslim call to prayer. None of us could sleep."

At 1 a.m., Capt. Toller and his men sat on the roof of the Pakistani quarters and waited. The AC130 gunship had gone ahead of them. They were so close to the fighting, shrapnel showered their compound from the gunship's 105mm shells. EOD's first and primary responsibility would be to clear booby traps and unexploded friendly and enemy shells. They also had to be prepared to check captured weapons and munitions and, if necessary, blow holes in the compound walls to allow the Pakistanis to assault the defenses of Aideed's fighters.

"I'd like to pray for you again," Capt. Toller told his men. Opening the tattered pages of his Bible, Steve prayed Psalm 91 and Isaiah 54:17 as prayers of protection.

By 4 a.m., Steve and his men were ready. Slipping through the gates to enter the battle, grenade fragments rained on their heads.

"The fighting was so intense," Steve says, "that I felt like I'd stepped into a scene from a war movie. Cobra gunships came in firing just above our heads. We took heavy fire, but managed to penetrate a wall and cleared the area of booby traps. Terrorists, breaking out to the north toward the Moroccan contingent, used their own women and children as human shields while they threw grenades."

Hours later, the grisly scene ended with a heavy death toll in the Moroccan division. There were 45 Moroccans dead, including their battalion commander, and one Pakistani soldier was killed and others wounded in the immediate vicinity of Steve and his men. No injuries in the EOD.

Passing the Word

In July, Steve Toller received orders sending him and his men home. Another EOD unit would be assigned to replace them.

During their tour of duty in Somalia, Capt. Steve Toller and his men of the EOD had destroyed 150 tons of munitions, 5,000 weapons, weapon systems, tanks and anti-aircraft guns. They had responded to 250 incidents by defusing or destroying unexploded land mines, bombs and grenades. Many of these while under fire.

Yet not one man in the group was killed, wounded or became ill during the ordeal.

When Toller met with the officer who would replace him in Somalia, he briefed him on the situation, reviewing military logs. After he finished, he took a moment to look in the other man's eyes. Then, slowly, carefully, he told him about bombs, about sniper fire, about people dying on every side, and how no harm had touched his men.

Finally, Toller took a deep breath and told him about the most incredible secret weapon ever used in a military campaign. A weapon that had never been beaten or destroyed. A weapon that was more powerful than the atom bomb. A weapon that had been launched by an ancient king named David. A weapon that had protected men from Hitler, Stalin and now from Gen. Aideed.

Capt. Toller scanned the landscape. It was quiet. Too quiet. He could feel the hair raise at the back of his neck. *Snipers.* He sensed their presence as surely as the mosquitoes that buzzed incessantly around him. Mosquitoes and snipers had a lot in common. They both wanted blood—his blood, and the blood of his men. Steve's goal was to thwart their mission.

Capt. Toller passed on his command, and now his protection. Opening his shirt pocket, he pulled out the Bible he'd carried there for months. Pressing the Bible into the man's outstretched hand, Steve Toller passed on the best kept secret in the military today.

The spoken Word of God.
Code Name: Prayer.

Editor's Note: The officer who replaced Steve Toller in Somalia reported back to him that he'd prayed the same scriptures and he, too, returned without losing a man.

On January 26, 1994, Capt. Steve Toller was awarded the Bronze Star for his service in Somalia.

When the Earth Shakes

by Melanie Hemry

Editor's Note:

In January of 1994, Southern California shook under the devastating power of one of the worst earthquakes in recent years. While many Christians did experience loss and damage, we believe the following story of the members of Thousand Oaks Christian Fellowship will build your faith and encourage you regarding God's protection.

Thursday, January 13, 1994— Thousand Oaks, California

Brenda Steen stepped into the sanctuary of Thousand Oaks Christian Fellowship and sighed with contentment. Although there were no services today, no loving faces and happy voices to greet her, the silent sanctuary was warm and inviting.

Brenda, alongside her husband, Arland, had started this church 13 years ago. In those years, they had seen lives changed...families grow stronger in the Lord...children raised on the Word of God. Brenda sat on the steps of the altar praying, her heart rejoicing over all God had done here.

Yet even as she rejoiced, a sense of caution stirred in her heart. *What is it, Lord?*

In answer, she heard the gentle voice of the Holy Spirit speak the words He'd been saying repeatedly to her in recent days.

Make much of the blood.

It was a phrase full of meaning for Brenda. Months

before, she had listened enthralled, as her friend, Billye Brim, had described the revelation God had given her about the blood of Jesus. When Billye taught her message at Eagle Mountain International Church (located on the grounds of KCM), Brenda had asked for copies of the tapes and listened to them three times. Then she began the laborious task of transcribing each tape.

In December, 1993, she'd begun teaching the series each Sunday night. She was still teaching the series, but this week, for some reason, there seemed to be a fresh urgency about it. Day in and day out, the Holy Spirit kept reminding her, *Make much of the blood.*

Prompted by the Lord, Brenda began to pray, her words echoing through the sanctuary. "Father, I plead the blood of Jesus over this building...."

Sunday, January 16, 1994

Pastor Brenda Steen stepped in the podium to preach. Tonight's message would be "The Blood of the Passover Lamb: The Protecting Power of the Blood."

"I taught a great deal from Exodus 12," Brenda explains. "About how the Israelites were instructed to take a lamb for *each household.* The head of the household dipped the hyssop branch in the blood and applied it to the doorpost. They weren't to leave the house till morning. In other words, they were to *stay under the blood.*

"Verse 23 says that when the Lord saw the blood He wouldn't allow the destroyer to come into their house and strike them. I reminded the congregation how saints in years past used that same principle to pray a line of protection around their property by pleading the blood of Jesus."

"Satan the destroyer is hard at work in the earth today," Brenda declared. "Sometimes the destruction he brings takes the form of natural catastrophes. But if we will by faith apply the blood, those catastrophes will not touch us!"

"After the sermon, we were directed by the Holy Spirit to take communion," Arland says. "Instead of taking it as a congregation, the head of each household led the communion for their own family, praying a blood line of protection over each family member and their property."

That night before the service was over, Brenda Steen said something the members of Thousand Oaks Christian Fellowship would never forget. She said it didn't matter that they lived in California. It didn't even matter if they lived right *over a fault-line*. "Your family is safe because the blood of Jesus has been applied to your household. A blood line has been drawn."

Monday, January 17, 1994, 4:31 A.M.

In the darkest hour of the night, while Southern California slept, a previously unknown fault-line erupted, changing the course of lives and the course of geology forever. The earthquake measured 6.8 on the Richter scale producing a power so great it pushed two mountain ranges higher and closer together, and depressed the valley between them by four inches.

Sixty-one people perished due to the earthquake as megastructures collapsed and highways broke apart like toy building blocks. Original estimates placed the cost of the destruction somewhere between $15 billion and $30 billion. It may prove to be the most costly natural disaster in the nation's history.

Those who survived the earthquake faced a myriad of problems: homelessness...isolation...loss of electricity...loss of water...broken gas lines...fires...and, in the weeks to come, 2,000 aftershocks, some measuring as high as 5.5 on the Richter scale.

Thousand Oaks, California, was declared a national disaster area. But the members of Thousand Oaks Christian Fellowship made a different declaration. For, when the earthquake was over, each one of them had a story of victory to tell.

"Nothing Was Broken!"

Stuart Schlosser awoke to the shaking and rolling that could only mean one thing—earthquake!

"My first thought was that we had nothing to worry about because the night before we'd prayed for a blood line around the house. But as I bolted out of bed, I heard my children praying a blood covering over my business. *My business!* I hadn't even thought about *it.*"

At 9:30 that morning, Stuart left home to try and make his way to his Subway Shop located in Northridge. He didn't know then that Northridge sat over the epicenter of the earthquake. He didn't know that a scant mile and a half from his business, one whole floor of the Northridge Meadows Apartments had collapsed killing 16 people. He didn't know that the University of California at Northridge science building—across the street from his business—had burned and half the dormitories had been destroyed.

"There was a strange glow in the sky," Stuart recalls, "and parts of the expressway were missing. Squad cars surrounded the exit I always took to work.

"All the windows were gone in the Kentucky Fried Chicken near my shop," Stuart recalls. "Every other window was missing from the shopping center. The doors to businesses next to mine were tilted and broken. Then I pulled up to the Subway Shop. Every window was intact. The doors were intact. Inside, bread racks had moved and food had fallen off the shelves in the refrigerator. A couple of ceiling tiles had fallen.

"Nothing was broken. Not a mirror, not a dish. I didn't even lose one light bulb."

"There Was No Fear!"

Keith Wengler's shift at UPS began that morning at 4:30. Keith was standing next to the conveyor belt waiting for packages when the earthquake exploded underneath him.

Panic-stricken people ran in every direction. Some rushed for the door while others hid under the belt. The building shook with a deafening roar. Outside, trucks clanked together. Keith had lived through earthquakes before, but without question this was the worst he'd ever experienced.

In spite of the turmoil around him, Keith could think of only one thing. *My family! What's happening at home?*

"Just as suddenly as that thought flashed through my mind," Keith says, "I remembered the blood. I prayed for my family. There was no fear. None, whatsoever. I drove home in peace."

When he arrived, Keith found his house and family safe and secure. Although the earth beneath them had trembled and shaken violently, it had succeeded only in moving one picture and knocking over the teddy bear collection that belonged to Keith's wife, Leigha.

"Everything was perfectly intact," Leigha says. "We were protected by the blood!"

"...An Angel Set My Home Down!"

"I woke up at 4:31 a.m.," recalls Jennifer Clark. "My waterbed was thrown up off the floor and half of my mobile home was in the air. I *screamed,* 'In the Name of Jesus, I pray the blood of Jesus over my children, myself and my house!'"

Instantly, the house settled back in place.

"Then I heard my little daughter, Christina, shout, 'I plead a blood ring around this whole park!'

"The next morning I saw indentations in a perfect line marking where the trailer had lifted on one end and wrinkled the metal. I believe when I prayed an angel set my home back down."

Fifty to 90 percent of all homes in mobile home parks were devastated. Yet, in Jennifer Clark's mobile home park, only three were lost. Jennifer believes that those three were damaged first, but all the others were protected by the blood of the Lamb and the word of Christina's testimony.

"Our Home Became a Peaceful Refuge."

Juanita Pryor's house was shaking violently when she awoke that Monday morning. "I could hear things falling in every room," she recalls. Yet instead of cringing in fear or fleeing in terror, Juanita boldly stood her ground. "Something rose up in me and I started yelling, 'The blood of Jesus! I cover this house with the blood of Jesus!'

"We gathered the family and sang songs about the blood for a long time before we checked the damage. I have a lot of pictures and glass things all over the house and most of them had fallen."

But nothing was broken. Nothing.

"I believe angels caught my things and placed them on the floor. Our home became a peaceful refuge for another family who needed a place to stay. When my friend walked in she said, 'I can relax now.'"

God Hath Remembered

Aftershocks and violent crime continued to rock the area for weeks after the first quake. Yet even though the danger wore on, the power of the blood didn't wear out. On January 26, nine days after the earthquake, Larry and Suzi Fox discovered that fact for themselves.

The Fox house was quiet as Suzi turned out the lights and prepared for bed that night. She didn't expect Larry home from work until late. As the general manager of a restaurant—the only one in its chain that had remained open since the quake—he had been extremely busy in recent days.

At 11 p.m., Suzi made her usual bedtime check on Chelsea, their 2-year-old. Walking into the bedroom, she was surprised to see Chelsea's wide eyes staring back at her.

How strange. Chelsea isn't usually awake at this time of night. Her spirit suddenly alert, Suzi sensed the warning of the Holy Spirit. *Something's wrong. Larry is in trouble!*

"Chelsea," she said, "we need to pray for Daddy." Without hesitation, Suzi prayed the blood of Jesus over Larry and called forth angels to protect him. Then she picked up her Bible and prayed Psalm 91, "Father, I thank You that Larry abides under the shadow of the Almighty...."

At 11:15 p.m., Larry was working quietly in his office at the restaurant, finishing up the day's accounts. The restaurant doors were locked, both safes closed and secured for the night.

Suddenly Larry's office door crashed to the floor as two gunmen stormed in upon him. "Get to the floor!" screamed one of them, holding a pistol to Larry's head.

"Let's kill 'em now!" shouted the other as he shoved two of Larry's co-workers into his office at gunpoint.

Larry lay on the floor with an astounding sense of peace. Praying in tongues under his breath, he listened to the gunmen with calm—until he heard them say something that sent chills down his spine.

"We'll put them in the freezer," one gunman said.

"Oh God, not the freezer!" Larry knew their walk-in freezer was equipped with an internal mechanism allowing the door to be unlocked from the inside. But that mechanism had been broken in the earthquake.

"There were two safes visible," Larry explains. "Most of the money was in the upper safe, but they acted like they couldn't see that one. They told me to open the lower safe."

Larry crawled to the safe and opened it, trying to anticipate their next move. Shockingly enough, there was no "next move." The gunmen simply grabbed the money and left, leaving Larry and the cooks completely unharmed.

Six days after the robbery, Suzi Fox gave birth to their second child—a son. They named him Zachary, which means *God hath remembered.*

"The Lord Made a Difference."

Although each story of victory is precious, what is most striking about the experiences of those at Thousand Oaks Christian Fellowship is their consistency. These are not isolated incidents. The testimonies reported here could be repeated by every member of Thousand Oaks Christian Fellowship for *not one of them lost a life or lost a home in the earthquake or its aftermath.*

Perhaps even more importantly, they didn't lose the peace and security in their families. Unlike the thousands of California children who were so shaken by the earthquake that they required psychiatric help, many of the children from the Steens' church ended up more confident in God's protection than ever before.

After one strong aftershock, for instance, 4-year-old Justin Riddle ran to his mother and said, "Mommy, did you feel the earth shake?"

"Yes, I did," Donna Riddle answered. "Were you afraid?"

"Naw..." shrugged Justin, "I just pleaded the blood."

Justin is too young to know his response to the earthquake is different from that of many other children. But it is...and Pastors Brenda and Arland Steen are thrilled about it.

"When the time of calamity came to the land of Egypt during Moses' day, the Lord made a difference between the Egyptians and the Israelites," Arland says. "As time moves forward in these last days there'll be earthquakes, famines, wars and rumors of wars. But there will always be a difference between the world and the Church."

That difference will be the blood of Jesus. And it will stand firm even when the earth itself shakes with uncertainty. The members of Thousand Oaks Christian Fellowship are rock-solid sure about that.

Arland and Brenda have been Partners with Kenneth Copeland Ministries for 19 years!

CHAPTER 3

Testimonies of Healing

"My Son, attend to my words;
consent and submit to my sayings.
Let them not depart from your sight;
keep them in the center of your heart.
For they are life to those who find them,
healing and health to all their flesh.
Keep your heart with all vigilance and above all
that you guard, for out of it flow the springs of life.
Put away from you false and dishonest speech,
and willful and contrary talk
put far from you."

Proverbs 4:20-24, The Amplified Bible

No Petal in Heaven's Garden

by Melanie Hemry

March 23, 1990, was one of those dreamy days in rural Tennessee when the sun lures a man outside with the inviting promise of summer. To Riley Walker Jr. it seemed almost picture-book perfect.

He could think of nowhere he'd rather be than here in the country, 40 miles from his Nashville home, enjoying a peaceful afternoon with those he loved most. Leaning against a maple tree, he surveyed the scene around him. His gaze swept past beautiful trees, glistening ponds and horses grazing nearby... then rested on his family. His wife, Beverly, their three sons, 7-year-old Riley III, 6-year-old Brandon and 3-year-old Michael, huddled happily together at the water's edge, laughing and taking turns fishing with an old cane pole. Beverly's grandmother, Dolly, rested in a lawn chair nearby.

For hours they'd tried to catch the catfish that swam lazily around the bottom of the pond. The catfish, fat and well-fed, had ignored the worm dangling from their cane pole, but little brim had begun biting so fast, the kids were pulling in one fish after another. Riley closed his eyes against the morning sun and thought that the sound of his children's laughter was the most beautiful sound on earth.

"We stayed until the last worm was gone," Riley remembers. "Then Brandon raced his older brother up the hill to the fence. I followed them while Beverly and her grandmother gathered our things."

That day, for the first time in all his six years, little Brandon beat his brother in a race. Eyes dancing, he fell giggling against the fence.

"The man who gave me permission to fish on that land asked us not to open the gate," Riley explains. "So I lifted Brandon over the fence. He was about to run across the road to our van when I heard the sound of a car or truck. I couldn't see anything because the road was hilly, but I knew something was moving toward us fast. I yelled, 'Brandon, wait!'"

Obediently, Brandon stopped in his tracks beside the road and waited as a truck topped the hill and sped past. Thinking all was clear, Brandon darted into the road. But the roar of the truck rushing by had masked the sound of a second vehicle.

Riley looked up to see a half-ton Chevrolet truck top the hill at high speed. Before he had time to yell a warning, the truck hit his son, flinging his twisted body 20 feet into the air.

Beverly dropped the lawn chair in her hand when she heard the sound of one agonized word that seemed to tear itself from her husband's heart.

"Brandon!"

Riley jumped the fence and ran to the ditch where his son's shattered body lay. An ex-Marine, Riley had been trained in every form of emergency situation. He knew CPR, and he knew the special considerations when giving CPR to a child. But one look at his son's body sent forth a wave of shock that almost drove that knowledge from his mind.

Still. He lay so utterly still. Sightless eyes stared into space. Riley dropped beside him, placing fingers under Brandon's nose to feel for breath. *Nothing.* He lowered his cheek to Brandon's face to feel or hear him breathing, praying for something...anything. *Nothing.* He felt the carotid artery in Brandon's neck for a pulse. *Nothing.* He placed a hand on Brandon's heart, hoping to feel a flutter. *Nothing.* He looked at Brandon's twisted chest. It looked so frail and broken. Would CPR press broken bones into his heart or lungs?

Seeing the apparent hopelessness of his son's condition, Riley had already begun to think about calling the police and planning a funeral. When the teenager who'd driven the truck that hit Brandon anxiously ran up and asked, "How's your son?" Riley answered, "My son is dead."

The young man fell, sobbing, onto the ground.

"I tried to make myself think," Riley recalls, "but all I heard were those words, *my son is dead.*"

But Riley's thoughts were interrupted by a scripture that he'd planted in his heart. Nudging aside visions of coffins and flowers, the power of that word that came up from within his spirit snapped him back to reality.

"Let this mind be in you, which was also in Christ Jesus" (Philippians 2:5).

"I kept hearing that verse over and over until it caught my attention," Riley says. "Finally I began to wonder how Jesus' mind would work in a situation like this. He'd never lost a son, but his friend, Lazarus died. Of course, Jesus raised him from the dead after four days. He'd said, 'Lazarus! Come forth!' But could I do such a thing?"

As if in answer, a second scripture rose up from Riley's heart.

"Verily, verily, I say unto you, He that believeth on me, the works that I do shall he do also; and greater works than these shall he do; because I go unto my Father" (John 14:12).

In that instant, Riley Walker knew what he had to do. He remembered that Jesus often referred to those who were dead as merely sleeping. Kneeling beside his son, he lay both hands on Brandon's head.

"Brandon! In the Name of Jesus, wake up!"

Nothing.

"Brandon! In the Name of Jesus, wake up!"

Another moment of silence. Then Brandon coughed and began a faint, gurgling respiration.

"I'd sent the driver of the first truck to call an ambulance," Riley explains. "Now I looked up and saw him knocking on the door of the house nearby. My son was breathing and he needed help fast. I knew those people weren't home, and we didn't have time to drive to the nearest town for help."

Riley, leaving his son, gathered up all his 140 pounds and ran toward the house. "Get out of the way!" he shouted to the teenager still knocking on the door. When Riley hit that door, he hadn't counted on the power of the Holy Spirit behind him. The force of the blow knocked the door off all its hinges. The door hit the floor with Riley on top of it, and slid across the room. The door—and Riley—skidded to a stop in front of the telephone.

When the teenager ran up and asked, "How's your son?" Riley answered, "My son is dead." "I tried to make myself think," Riley recalls, "but all I heard were those words, *my son is dead.*"

"When the ambulance arrived," Beverly recalls, "my jeans were soaked with the blood from Brandon's head injury. The ambulance attendant didn't think he'd live long enough to make it to the hospital, and didn't want me to ride with them. I wouldn't back down. Finally, they let me ride next to the driver."

"You just don't understand how badly your son is hurt," one medic told Beverly. "You're just lucky he's alive."

"I'm not lucky he's alive," Beverly said. "I'm blessed."

"Well, you need to face the facts. Your son weighs 50 pounds. He was hit by a full-size truck at high speed. *If* he makes it at all, you're probably looking at a year and a half in the hospital...brain damage...paralysis."

The medic didn't realize it, but he'd just helped Beverly plan her prayer for the ride back to Nashville. She prayed against paralysis, brain damage and a long hospital stay. Nearing the hospital, she heard more.

"ETA...5 minutes," the driver called.

"We won't make it!" the medic yelled, "we're losing him!"

Beverly turned in her seat and shouted, "Brandon! I'm here with you. In the Name of Jesus, hold on! We're almost there! Don't give up!"

Brandon clung to life as the ambulance screamed into the hospital parking lot. While Brandon was rushed into the emergency room, Beverly called to activate their church intercessory prayer group.

Memories flashed through Beverly's mind while she waited. Brandon bringing her flowers. He didn't bring her weeds. He went to the neighbor's house and picked roses and irises. When she scolded him, Brandon said, "But you're so pretty, I want to give you pretty flowers."

"I felt like I was losing a grip on my emotions," Beverly says. "I went to the bathroom to pray alone. All I could think was that I couldn't live without Brandon. I didn't care if he were brain damaged or paralyzed. I just wanted him alive. I was about to open my mouth to pray, when the Holy Spirit interrupted."

No! Don't compromise!

Beverly realized she'd almost fallen into the devil's trap. Instead, she prayed, "Father, I know that I don't have to compromise with You. You are able. I receive Brandon alive and whole. I thank You that he'll be whole in every way."

The Walkers waited. Occasionally, they heard a report.

"The brain scan showed no bleeding."

"We scanned his stomach...no bleeding."

Once, Riley, Beverly and her sister walked around the back hall and listened outside the door while three doctors discussed Brandon's spinal X-rays. *Right here...fracture of the neck...paralysis.*

Riley and Beverly joined hands and prayed against a broken neck and paralysis. Later, they were told the tests were inconclusive. The only thing they knew for sure was that Brandon's right arm was broken in two places and he was in a coma. They set his arm and moved him to the intensive care unit.

As they waited for Brandon to get out of intensive care, their pastor came to the hospital. Though he was tempted to worry, God had given him peace, instructing him to pray against brain damage and paralysis—the same thing the ambulance driver had told Beverly.

"It was hours before we got to see Brandon," Beverly remembers. "The waiting room was filled with all kinds of grief. My friend, Marilyn, was distressed. She'd been talking to other families. One 12-year-old girl had a brain stem tumor and was going blind.

A baby had a hole in its heart and would have to be operated on. And the doctors said if one little boy went into distress again, they were going to 'pull the plug.'"

When Marilyn recounted the horrors to Beverly, fire flashed from her eyes. "Look, Marilyn," she declared, "Brandon is going to be all right. And so are those other kids. Satan has messed with the wrong child this time!"

Satan soon learned the truth of those words.

Marilyn and Beverly prayed for each child. When they prayed for the boy whose doctor was about to 'pull the plug,' Beverly felt like she was hitting a spiritual wall. That boy's mother looked haggard, gray and lifeless. The next afternoon Beverly understood the resistance to her prayers.

Beverly listened while good, well-meaning church members comforted that mother.

"God needs him more than you do."

"That's right. He is a petal in God's rose garden."

"You've had him almost nine years, now God needs him back. You've got to accept this."

When the visitors were gone, that mother asked Beverly how Brandon was doing.

"I told her he was better," Beverly recalls. "I said it by faith. He didn't *look* better. He was in a coma with tubes in his arms, nose and throat.

"The lady said I was lucky Brandon was better. I told her I was blessed by God, and that He'd do the same for her son. She turned and walked away like she'd been slapped. Later, I apologized for offending her, but testified to God's desire to heal. She said I just didn't know what they'd been through." But Beverly continued to pray.

While Brandon lay in a coma, the report came back. The baby with a hole in its heart had experienced a change. The surgery had been canceled. When the girl with the brain tumor asked for a minister to pray for her, the family asked Riley Walker. He prayed the prayer of faith for her healing.

During Brandon's second day in ICU, he woke up from his coma. Three days after the accident, he was moved to a regular room. On Friday, one week after being hit by a truck, Brandon was discharged from the hospital.

"We won't make it!" the medic yelled, "We're losing him!" Beverly turned in her seat and shouted, "Brandon! I'm here with you. In the Name of Jesus, hold on!"

"I couldn't believe they were letting him out of the hospital so soon," Beverly says. "The day before he'd spoken his first word, and he still couldn't walk. The doctors said he'd have to learn to walk again. They sent him home with a wheelchair and ordered nurses and an occupational therapist to come by every day."

Brandon had an instinctive hatred of the wheelchair. He refused to sit in it. His brothers played in it and raced it around the house, but Brandon would have no part of it. The day he arrived home, a therapist arrived to measure his legs and start his exercises. He couldn't straighten his leg because of muscle damage. She said it would take months of therapy to undo the damage.

"On Saturday," Beverly remembers, "I started doing the exercises on Brandon's leg. I'd been praying for patience before the accident, and I was about to pray for patience during this long process when the

Holy Spirit interrupted me again. Instead, I sat there massaging his leg for a while, then asked God to straighten and heal it. The leg straightened out that day and he slowly started walking.

"On Monday, the therapist came back. She said if she hadn't seen Brandon and done the measurements herself, she wouldn't believe it was the same patient."

One week after his discharge from the hospital, Brandon was taken back to have his arm checked. The girl with the brain tumor was so much better she was being moved out of ICU. The boy who'd been so critical was now in a regular room. Beverly saw his mother talking to the doctors. She was rosy-cheeked and smiling.

"All of a sudden, I knew for sure why Brandon got out of the hospital so fast," Beverly says. "Satan was terrified to let him stay."

Two weeks after his discharge from the hospital, Brandon returned to see his doctor. "I'd like to take credit for this," the doctor said, after examining Brandon, "but you folks have had a miracle."

"I kept Brandon home from school with a tutor for a week," Beverly says. "But the following week were the T-Cap exams. No child could pass to the next grade without taking those tests. Brandon went back to school, taking the tests with his left hand. The teachers didn't expect him to do well with his recent head injury, but he passed with flying colors."

That spring, Beverly cried when she took the boys to the park. "The sheer joy of watching him run and play and seeing his eyes dance and sparkle was overwhelming," Beverly recalls.

Brandon sang a solo and danced in the Christmas pageant that year. Today, he is an honor student, plays baseball, basketball and loves to race his brother.

Regular viewers of *Believer's Voice of Victory* broadcasts, Riley and Beverly Walker had planted the Word of God in their hearts every day. When trouble struck and they had no time to stop and study, that planted Word caused them to put on the mind of Christ, instead of the mind of crisis.

As a result, their son isn't a petal in God's heavenly garden. He's growing and prospering right where he was planted—here on earth, a living testimony to the power of God's spoken Word.

Update: According to Brandon's mom, he has continued to be blessed and be a blessing. He has been on the honor roll several times, received awards for academic excellence and won first place in a speech competition at his school. He plays basketball, baseball and recently won first place at the State Junior Olympics in the 400-meter, 800-meter and 4 x 400-meter relay team.

Riley and Beverly have been Partners with Kenneth Copeland Ministries for 4 years!

Countdown to a Miracle

by Melanie Hemry

March 1991—Donelle Moore walked from room to room praying peace over her four sleeping daughters, Olivia, Sarah, Diana and Elisha. Locking all the doors, she crawled into her own bed. As she drifted off to sleep, Donelle slipped, it seemed, into another world—a dream world where the stillness of her bedroom was shattered by a raging storm.

It was there, standing in that dream world with her nightgown whipping furiously in the wind, that she first saw it. An angry black mass rushing toward her on the horizon. A monstrous pitch enveloping everything in its path.

Even in her dreams, Donelle knew how to respond to such a threat. She fell prostrate on the floor and began to pray in the Holy Spirit.

But the boiling black cloud still bore down on her. Coming closer and closer with each passing second. Suddenly, the voice of the Holy Spirit spoke in her. His words brought instant peace.

Do what you know to do, He said.

Instantly, Donelle awoke.

"I went to my pastor with the dream," Donelle remembers. "He told me there was a great battle coming, but I would be victorious over it."

That same month, an evangelist held a revival in the Moores' church. Asking Donelle's 16-year-old daughter, Olivia, to stand, he prophesied these words over her: "The devil is bidding a high price for your life. But there will be a day when you will stand up and prophesy. Your words will be like burning coals on the lips of the people."

Donelle understood clearly, after the dream and the prophecy over Olivia, that a battle was brewing. "I told my prayer partner that if the devil was stupid enough to make a play for me or my family, I would whip him with the blood of Jesus like he hadn't been whipped since Calvary," she said.

Was she bluffing? Satan would soon find out.

Wednesday, May 22, 1991—Donelle stood during the praise and worship service singing and magnifying the Name of Jesus. A while later she had the uncanny sense of someone watching her. Glancing into the aisle, she saw Him. Jesus. He met her gaze and asked simply, *Are you ready?*

Looking into His eyes, Donelle was transported to a place of total peace. With Him at her side how could she lose? "Yes," she told Him, "I'm ready."

Friday, May 24, 1991—Donelle looked at the clock. 4:45 p.m. Time to start dinner. Humming softly to herself she remembered to set one less plate than usual. Olivia had gone to the beach at Lake Fenton with friends. As Donelle reached toward the cupboard, she was jarred by the unexpected jangle of the telephone.

"Do you have a daughter named Olivia?" the caller asked.

"Yes...."

"We have your daughter at the hospital. Do you have a car?"

"Yes, what's wrong with my daughter?"

"Would you come to the hospital immediately?"

"Is she alive?"

"Just come."

Donelle still clutched the phone after the line went dead. She felt shrouded by a mass of terrible blackness. She couldn't see...or think. Fear rose in her throat.

Do what you know to do.

The words jolted Donelle into action. She called her other daughters to her side to pray with her.

"Father," she cried, "Olivia's been hurt and I ask You in Jesus' Name to heal her. If she's dead, I expect You to raise her up. Olivia's protection is covered in my covenant with You, and I am calling on that covenant today."

Once the prayer was prayed, the outcome settled, Donelle turned on her adversary with a vengeance. "Satan, my child is under the blood of Jesus in Whose Name I speak. You can't have her, *or any part of her!"*

It would take weeks to piece together the scene that took place on Lake Fenton that day. But bit by bit, the facts came in. Olivia had been riding in a boat with six teenagers. Three boys rode in front. Four girls in back. The boat went into a power slide, fast, making a 180-degree turn. All four girls fell out. Only three of them surfaced.

The terrified boys pulled the girls into the boat. They all searched the water for a glimpse of Olivia. What they finally saw made them sick.

Pieces of flesh and bone floated on the now calm water.

Suddenly, Olivia surfaced beside the boat. As the boys tried to pull her in, her agonized screams echoed to the shore. The propeller had chopped its way up her right leg. What was left of the leg was attached by a shred of skin on her inner thigh.

Miraculously, two men arrived on the scene to help. They said a man in a 30-foot tuna boat had sent them.

A tuna boat on Lake Fenton? No one else had seen it.

"When I arrived at the emergency room," Donelle explains, "I asked again if Olivia was alive. They said, 'Yes...for now.'"

The doctor drew Donelle aside to tell her that Olivia's injuries were very serious.

"Do you think you can save her leg?" Donelle asked.

"Ma'am," he answered quietly, "we don't even know if we can save her life."

Donelle listened as the doctor explained that 5 inches of the bone and muscle were missing from Olivia's thigh. Tests would be performed to determine if the veins and arteries were strong enough to save. If not, they couldn't even attempt surgery.

Donelle looked at the X-rays of her daughter's leg. It didn't take a medical degree to see that there wasn't much left. It looked more like a scrambled jigsaw puzzle than human bone. Surrounded by doctors, nurses and technicians, Donelle stretched her hands toward the X-ray film and spoke. "In the Name of Jesus, I command each piece of bone to move into place and be whole! Arteries you will be whole! Veins you will be whole! I command you to come into line with the Word of God!" The medical staff stepped back respectfully as Donelle walked away.

"I went to the waiting room," Donelle remembers. "The Spirit of God rose up with steel-like strength within me. I still didn't know how Olivia had been hurt and it didn't matter. I knew from my dream that my job was to humble myself before God and pray in the Spirit. Patients and visitors gathered in the lobby to watch television. I couldn't worry about that. I just kept praying in tongues. Family and friends arrived asking me questions. I told them I didn't have time to talk—I had work to do."

8:30 p.m.—Olivia was still alive. Nurses had nick-named her "Miracle Child." Test reports showed that the arteries and veins in Olivia's leg could withstand surgery. Two surgeons, weary from a long day, pre-pared for a surgery that would challenge the skill of any mortal man. Donelle stepped forward.

"May I pray over your hands?" Both doctors sighed gratefully and stretched out their hands to her.

"Father," Donelle prayed, "in the Name of Jesus, give them skill, knowledge and wisdom to do what they need to do." Grasping their hands, Donelle smiled encouragement to the men. "Just do what you know to do," she said simply. *"He'll do the rest."*

Midnight—Olivia had been in surgery for 2½ hours. Donelle had not ceased to pray in the Spirit. She knew without a doubt that Jesus of Nazareth—The Carpenter and Master Builder—was present in that lobby. He spoke strength to her spirit through the scriptures. *"I will contend with him that contendeth with thee, and I will save thy children"* (Isaiah 49:25).

"About midnight," Donelle recalls, "my prayers changed. Until then, I had sensed that I was in a war. Just fighting and pressing through. Now, with every word in my prayer language I heard victory. Jesus spoke to me and said, *Just watch and see what I'm going to do now!* It was the most excruciating, yet exciting, night of my life."

2 a.m.—The orthopedic surgeon walked into the waiting area with a smile. "We're finished with the bone," he said.

"How did it go?" Donelle asked.

"You already know, don't you?" he asked, grinning.

"I do," Donelle answered with a laugh, "but I'd like to hear you say it."

"Those bones," the doctor said, relishing the moment, "came together... *perfectly.*"

Still, the surgery was far from over. Now doctors began the tedious task of piecing together muscle.

9 a.m.—The surgery team staggered out of the operating room in exhaustion. Olivia had been under an anesthetic for almost 12 hours. Doctors and nurses had worked all night with no sleep, standing for hours on cold, hard tile floors. Everything humanly possible had been done.

Donelle sat beside Olivia's bed in the intensive care unit. For the first time since her ordeal had begun, Donelle stopped praying and rested her head on the bed beside her daughter's unconscious form. She thought about the strange pattern of events. The dream, the prophecy, the vision. Those words, *Do what you know to do.* She *had* known what to do.

Suddenly, Olivia surfaced beside the boat. As the boys tried to pull her in, her agonized screams echoed to the shore.

She remembered back to when Olivia was a baby. Back then Donelle had known more about the do's and don'ts of religion than about the Man Jesus. Then one morning the radio alarm switched on at 5:30 a.m. and all that began to change.

"A preacher came on the radio," Donelle explains, "who sounded like he was having fun. He said the devil would scream and tell you he was going to tear you from limb to limb, but he was nothing but a little old liar with a great big mouth."

That preacher was Kenneth Copeland. Donelle had climbed out of bed laughing that morning and determined to tune in to his broadcast again. Now, 16 years later, she was saved, filled with the Holy Spirit and knew for herself the truth of Brother Copeland's words.

When Olivia woke up, she told her mother about the amazing experience she'd had on the lake that day. "When I fell out of the boat I felt the propeller cut up my leg," she explained. "The ski ropes wrapped themselves around my arms. I was totally bound. I couldn't hold my breath any longer and I screamed, "Jesus!" When I said that Name I breathed in air—no water—just pure fresh air. Later, I felt someone pull the ski ropes over my head like a sweater. Then I felt hands around my waist lifting me out of the water."

Donelle looked at Olivia and smiled. A fragment of the scripture she'd clung to these past 24 hours came once again to her mind...*and I will save your children.*

A while later, the pulmonary specialist came in with a puzzled expression on his face. "We might as well turn this oxygen off," he said. "I don't understand it, but there isn't any water in her lungs. In fact, there never has been."

Doctors anticipated that Olivia would stay in the hospital for four months before she could be discharged and start rehabilitation. They said if she walked again it would be with a limp and a foot brace. Donelle refused to agree with that report. Three weeks after the surgery Olivia was dismissed from the hospital.

Today, she attends high school and goes to the football games. She walks without crutches. The injured leg can support her full weight. She doesn't need a foot brace. She has no limp. Each X-ray is more amazing than the last. Pieces of her bones surely rest on the bottom of Lake Fenton. Yet, all the gaps in her thigh have grown together as the leg continues to mend. When Donelle told Satan he couldn't have any part of her daughter, she meant it.

The devil indeed bid a high price for Olivia Moore's life. But, the deck was stacked against him. He could never deal a hand of evil that would outmatch Jesus' blood. That blood was the price God had paid for Olivia. That blood made her a winner. And the winner takes all.

Update: Olivia recently completed studies at a university in Germany, enjoys downhill skiing, and has received many opportunities to share how God restored her body completely.

Donelle has been a Partner with Kenneth Copeland Ministries for 16 years!

A Lifetime Guarantee

by Melanie Hemry

Helen Jaeger picked up her purse, then stopped to check her lipstick in the mirror. The face that looked back at her radiated an energetic glow that made her look much younger than her 72 years. And why not? After all, the Bible promised one of the benefits of trusting God would be a renewed youth and Helen's trust in Him went back a very long time.

Looking at her watch, Helen grabbed her keys and headed down the hall. She didn't want to be late to her job as a volunteer receptionist at the church. She was feeling great. Then, suddenly the strength drained from her body. Dizzy, she felt the room spin as she groped for something to steady her. Shakily she made it to the sofa and collapsed.

Fifteen minutes later, the episode ended as quickly as it began.

It was probably nothing, reasoned Helen. After all, she'd enjoyed excellent health for years, walked briskly for exercise, and on any given trip to the mall, she could outlast and outshop her two daughters and even her five grandchildren. No doubt this incident would be an isolated occurrence.

It wasn't. The attacks recurred several times over the next two weeks, and in October of 1993 Helen's doctor asked her to check into a hospital just a few miles from her Tulsa, Oklahoma, home for tests. Oddly enough, one by one every test returned normal.

Home from the hospital, Helen called her daughters, Susan in Texas and Gina in Colorado, with the good news. "It's absolutely nothing to worry about," she told Gina.

Hanging up the phone, Gina sensed a strange heaviness in her heart. The voice of the Holy Spirit cut through the silence. His words echoing within her.

Don't be misled. Unless the course of things is changed, this sickness is unto death.

Never had Gina received such a warning from the Lord. She knew it wasn't God's will for her mother—or any other Christian—to be sick. As a writer for Kenneth Copeland Ministries, she'd learned that for sure. After listening to thousands of hours of the Copelands' tapes both on the job and at home, and studying the Word for herself, healing had become not just a scriptural doctrine to Gina, but a literal reality in her life.

At first, she'd combined her faith with doctors and medicine for faster more effective healing. But eventually, the Lord had instructed her to put her reliance totally on Him. Now, as Gina began to pray for her mother, she remembered the words He had spoken to her heart a few years ago.

There is coming a time when you will face diseases medical science cannot solve. You must begin to learn now to further develop your faith and walk in supernatural healing and health every day. If you don't, it will one day cost someone their life.

Gina had obeyed. Every day since then she had spoken healing scriptures aloud. Every time sickness lifted its head in her home, she smacked it down with the Word. As a result, it had been years since she or her children had needed doctors or medicine. God's power had been completely sufficient.

November and December passed uneventfully.

Helen had no more attacks and it appeared the tests were right. There was no need for alarm. Then in January the attacks began again. And this time they were vicious.

Now in addition to the weakness and dizziness, Helen's stomach and intestines were affected. Her heart rate sped up as high as 197 beats per minute. The attacks forced her into the hospital emergency room again and again. Often, by the time she arrived there, her body shook so violently the emergency room staff couldn't perform an electrocardiogram.

One evening, Helen experienced an attack so severe, the doctors feared it would precipitate a heart attack. In an effort to slow her racing heart, they gave her a dose of nitroglycerin. It didn't work.

A second dose of nitroglycerin was administered.

It didn't work either. In desperation, they gave her morphine.

Helen's grandson called Gina with a report. She hung up the phone with his words echoing in her mind. "It looks bad for Grandma. Please pray. I don't want her to die."

Gina had never felt so alone. Susan, her sister, was out of the country. Her husband, Jerry, was out of the state. She hadn't lived in Colorado long enough to make close friends. And although she'd been attending Happy Church in Denver for several months, she didn't yet know anyone she could ask to come and pray with her. Now her mother's life hung in the balance.

"I grabbed my Bible and crawled up into the middle of my bed," Gina remembers. "I'd just finished listening to Billye Brim's teaching on *The Overcoming Power of the Blood.* So I turned to the story of Rahab, the harlot. I meditated on that story for a while.

"Suddenly the truth of it hit me like a flash. Rahab saved the life of her entire family with a red rope that represented Jesus' blood. As a born-again, Spirit-filled Christian could I expect any less? I made a petition for my mother's life based on that same blood."

In Tulsa, Helen's heart rate slowed and the attack lifted as abruptly as it had occurred. Her doctor admitted her to the hospital for eight days of exhaustive tests. A well-known neurologist was called in on her case. It was he who finally discovered the problem.

"You have a condition which causes sudden drops in the serotonin level of your brain," he explained. "The drop in serotonin affects your central nervous system, which in turn affects every system in your body. That explains the violent shaking, the severe heart rates, the gastrointestinal involvement...everything you've experienced."

"How can the drops in serotonin be stopped?" Helen asked.

"Unfortunately, there is no cure," he answered. "The best we can do is control the symptoms by prescribing drugs that affect the entire central nervous system. The only drugs that do that are psychiatric drugs—antidepressants and tranquilizers."

"I was stunned by the news," Helen explains. "What choice did I have? The symptoms left unchecked would eventually destroy me—mind and body. But I'd seen the devastating effects of psychiatric drugs and I didn't want them either."

There was only one answer: divine healing.

Back home, Helen sat alone in her living room. It had been here in this very room she had first realized that healing was included in the redemption Jesus purchased through His death on the cross. For years, as a denominational Sunday school teacher she had taught that God sometimes healed and sometimes didn't. Then one day she had been reading about Jesus in Isaiah 53:4-5: *"Surely he took up our infirmities and carried our sorrows...and by his wounds we are healed" (New International Version).*

Helen had read those verses countless times, always assuming they referred only to spiritual healing, the cleansing of the heart from sin. But this time the Holy Spirit led her to Matthew 8:16-17: *"...and [Jesus] healed all the sick. This was to fulfill what was spoken through the prophet Isaiah: 'He took up our infirmities and carried our diseases'" (New International Version).* Helen's heart leapt. The New Testament itself interpreted Isaiah's words to include physical healing! That meant healing belonged to every Christian, just as surely as forgiveness of sin.

She had never again doubted God's will to heal. Even so, she realized now that she had never had to stand in faith in a situation this dangerous. And she knew she couldn't do it alone.

Helen called Gina and asked for help. "I need you to be my coach," she told her daughter. "I'll do whatever you tell me to do. Just come and help me tap into the supernatural power of God."

Gina packed her bags and flew to Tulsa.

"I was shocked when I arrived," Gina says. "My mother had always been the most upbeat person I'd ever known—even through my dad's death four years before. Now, when those attacks manifested, not only did her body shake as if in a seizure, her countenance darkened as if she were being pulled into a deep well of despair."

With each attack, Gina and her sister Susan laid hands on Helen and pled the precious blood of Jesus.

Each time the attack would stop within minutes. "That in itself was a great victory," Gina says, "but I knew she still wasn't healed."

Gina and Susan built their mother's faith by reading scriptures and books on healing aloud. When their voices tired, they played tapes of Gloria Copeland's *Healing School* and others.

"The attacks came less frequently, but when they did hit it was heart-wrenching to watch," Gina remembers. "We could be anywhere—sitting at the supper table or walking through a mall when it happened. A look of terror would cross Mom's face. *'Please help me,'* she'd whimper. Then she'd lose her ability to communicate. Her eyes would glaze over as she began to shake and she looked as though she didn't know who she was."

For two weeks, Gina and Susan prayed off one attack after another. Finally, Helen asked, "Can't I stand in faith *and* take the medicine?"

Both daughters shook their heads. "It won't work *in this case,*" they said. "The medicine will mask the symptoms but they'll also dull your mind. You must have your wits about you to fight this battle."

Just to be sure, Gina called a friend who is a Spirit-filled physician. He confirmed that there were no healing properties in those drugs. None. What's more, the drugs themselves were addictive and would eventually create further problems.

There was, however, one medicine Helen could take that *would* heal her. So Gina decided to put it in "prescription form." She selected specific scriptures and turned them into healing confessions. Then Helen wrote them on index cards so she could carry them with her constantly.

Helen took the first dose immediately. "The Word of God is life to me," she said, "and healing to all my flesh.

"God will strengthen me, and harden me to difficulties..."

From then on, Helen took her faith medicine several times a day and at the onset of each attack. "I couldn't remember my own name when an attack started," Helen remembers. "But Gina would get close to my face and start saying my scriptural affirmations. It took all my strength of will, but I'd finally repeat the words after her. At first it seemed to make no difference. But as I kept at it, I saw the power increase."

After two weeks together in Tulsa, Susan returned home to provide prayer support and Helen flew back to Colorado with Gina. Once there, Helen continued her diet of faith-building books and tapes. In addition, she and Gina began each day by reading the healing scriptures to each other from different versions of the Bible. That alone took an hour and a half, and often they did it twice a day.

"It was hard work," admits Helen. "The attacks were taking a heavy toll on my body. I'd lost weight. I'd lost physical strength. Even my face was thin and drawn. I was so tired that sometimes simple activities like getting dressed would leave me limp and breathless with exhaustion."

One morning she sat collapsed in a rocking chair after a particularly brutal attack. After it was over, she spoke, her voice little more than a whisper. "Can you promise me this is going to work?"

Gina thought of all the times God had proven His faithfulness in her household. How He had healed her family again and again. She knew that God Himself backed up His Word. It was a lifetime guarantee.

She looked her mother in the eye. "I *guarantee* you that the Word of God will work."

Sure enough, day by day, it did. As Helen became bolder in her confessions and her fight against the devil, the attacks became fewer and further between. Some days they didn't manifest at all.

The devil was clearly on the run, but both Gina and Helen were beginning to tire.

"One Wednesday night, Mom and I went to Happy Church. I could hardly wait to get there so I could get some rest from the battle," Gina says. "But during praise and worship that night an attack hit Mom. I saw her fall back across a chair, her face ashen. I knew what to do, but I couldn't find the strength to do it. I didn't even turn and look at her. I just started to cry."

Silently Gina began to pray, "Father, I'm making a heart cry to You. I'm crying in faith. Smith Wigglesworth said to stretch your faith as far as you can and then let God make up what's lacking with the nine gifts of the Spirit. Well, I'm stretched to the limit and I need one of those gifts right now."

Hanging up the phone, Gina sensed a strange heaviness in her heart. The voice of the Holy Spirit cut through the silence. His words echoing within her...*Don't be misled. Unless the course of things is changed, this sickness is unto death.*

Instantly, a man in the congregation stood, giving a message in tongues. When the associate pastor gave the interpretation, Gina wept again...this time, for joy.

The Lord says, I have heard the cry of your heart, and I know you're in a hard place. I know you have no more strength. But My strength picks up where yours ends.

Now you will see what I can do. And we will make it through to victory together.

Sobbing, Gina turned to her mother. Helen's color had returned to her face. Slowly, she stood to her feet. Gina and Helen stood in stunned silence. The attacks had started in October—six months ago. Never, in all that time, had an attack stopped spontaneously. Until now.

"I still had a few attacks attempt to manifest after that," Helen recalls, "but the power of the devil had been broken. My strength rose up, and I could use the Word of God to stop them before they started. I never had another manifestation of the disease."

The second week in April, Gina watched her mother board an airplane. Six weeks before, Helen couldn't go across the street alone. Now she was flying home to Tulsa. All by herself. Perfectly healed.

Today, Helen Jaeger's life has come full circle. She's back at work as a volunteer receptionist at her church. She teaches Sunday school, walks briskly most every day, and travels to visit her daughters and grandchildren. She is healthy, happy and enjoying her life to the fullest.

What about the disease that medical science couldn't cure? "It's gone..." says Helen, her eyes glistening with gratitude, "destroyed by the blood of the Lamb and the word of our testimony."

Will the Word of God destroy the yoke of bondage in your life?

Helen Jaeger's answer is bold and clear. "It will," she says. "I guarantee it."

Update: Helen is still active as ever and in excellent health!

Helen has been a Partner with Kenneth Copeland Ministries for 10 years!

In the Midst of the Cloud

by Melanie Hemry

Craig St. Ledger sensed a stirring of excitement when he left work on January 19, 1994. His job as a landscape worker at Kenneth Copeland Ministries wasn't glamorous, but Craig was glad to be a part of what God was doing there. In the past two days, ministers from all over the country had arrived for the Ministers' Conference at Eagle Mountain. It was a powerful gathering...and powerful things were sure to happen.

Craig's wife, Wanda, cautioned him to keep his guard up and resist the devil. "The devil hasn't got time for me," Craig stated. "He's after bigger bait." Bait, he thought, like Kenneth Copeland and Jesse Duplantis.

That evening Wanda watched her husband closely. Something felt...unsettled. It wasn't anything she could pin down. He'd just been different in some way the past few days. Excited about the conference. Indifferent about the devil. Tired...listless. *At least he's reading the Bible*, she thought, sliding into bed at 10 p.m. Even that seemed odd. For three hours straight, he'd read the book of Samuel. Now, when the phone rang, he asked *her* to get up and answer it!

Irritated, Wanda answered the phone. "Hello..."

The words on the other end of the line made the hair stand up on the back of her neck. *An obscene phone call.* Wanting the caller to know her husband was home, Wanda handed the telephone to Craig. Craig listened, spoke into the phone, then calmly hung up.

Seconds later, Craig St. Ledger—30-year-old husband and father of two small children—slumped over on the sofa. Dead.

"Craig?" Wanda looked closely at her husband. He gasped three times then lay perfectly still, his face a horrible ashen color. "Craig, stop it or I'll call 911!"

Nothing. Grabbing the telephone, Wanda dialed 911. *God, don't take him! My children!*

"Check to see if he's breathing," the voice on the telephone instructed. Wanda lay her hand on Craig's chest hoping to feel some movement. *Nothing.*

"Check to see if he has a pulse," the voice continued. Wanda unbuttoned Craig's shirt collar and felt for a pulse. *Nothing.* She felt his wrist. *Nothing.*

"Do you know how to do CPR?" the operator asked. Wanda stood still, horrified that her husband's life might hang on the answer she gave.

"No," she said, sobbing. "I don't know how."

Step by step, the voice on the telephone told Wanda what to do. Lay him flat on his back. Tilt his head back. Pinch his nose closed. Cover his mouth with your mouth. Take a deep breath through your nose. Blow the air into his mouth.

Suddenly a man and some women came to the house—they were paramedics who were visiting friends on our street. They had heard the call that was dispatched and were the first to arrive.

A Prayerful Vigil

Wanda's voice sounded hollow with pain when she called her parents. Somehow she choked out the words. "Craig's dead."

Police and ambulances arrived, and Wanda stood in the front yard, numb with shock. Suddenly a familiar, comforting sound penetrated her mind. *Prayer!* Turning, she saw a man standing in her yard praying in the Spirit. She walked over to him and asked, "Will you pray with me?"

Together, they prayed that Craig would not die, but live—totally healed.

"Our pastors, Allen and Beverly Shook, live across the street from us," Wanda explains. "They were at the Ministers' Conference at Eagle Mountain. The man who prayed with me was one of their friends, visiting from Michigan. When we finished praying, a peace flooded me that didn't make any natural sense.

"The paramedics worked on Craig, shocking his heart until it started beating again. But, he died again in the ambulance on the way to the hospital."

Again, Craig's heart was shocked to stimulate life. At the hospital, the doctor told Wanda that her husband was in a coma. He didn't know what was wrong with him, but he advised Craig's family to come quickly. The unspoken message was clear: Craig St. Ledger's frail grasp on life was slipping.

Word filtered to Allen and Beverly Shook that a member of their congregation was in critical condition. They left the Ministers' Conference and arrived at the hospital. Allen and Beverly kept a prayerful vigil beside Wanda for 48 hours. When Allen left to take care of church matters, Beverly stayed on, providing hope and faith for the weary family.

Meanwhile, news of Craig's condition reached Kenneth Copeland. He led 500 ministers in prayer for Craig St. Ledger to live and be healed.

"For the first two days, Craig's body convulsed with seizures," Wanda recalls. "The doctors said the convulsions were a result of brain damage. Although there had been some resuscitation during that time, Craig had been clinically dead for 20 minutes.

"To make matters worse, the jalapeño pizza he'd eaten for supper had emptied into his lungs causing pneumonia. Now a respirator forced air into his lungs through a tube down his throat.

"The tests showed he didn't have a heart attack, stroke, or an aneurysm. What he did have was a serious cardiac arrhythmia."

Day after day, Wanda sat beside Craig's bed and watched the rhythm of his heart march wildly across the monitor screen. Tall skinny beats raced across the screen, then huge, wide beats marched slowly like a mournful dirge. Turning her head away, she continued to pray and confess that by Jesus' stripes, Craig was healed.

"Go back!"

"As Craig came out of the coma," Wanda remembers, "he was restless and wanted out of the bed. The doctor said his electrocardiogram (EKG) showed scar tissue, which meant he may have had heart problems in the past and not known it. He said the arrhythmia caused Craig's heart to stop. He asked if Craig had ever blacked out. I remembered that he had blacked out once for about 10 seconds.

"They moved him to another hospital for more testing on the arrhythmia problem. Finally, they told us that Craig's condition would recur, and that the only way he would live is if we let them implant a permanent defibrillator. The device was designed to sense his arrhythmia and shock his heart back into rhythm when necessary."

Wanda felt that refusing the defibrillator would

affirm her faith that Craig was healed, but she didn't want to be presumptuous.

Finally, she got alone with God and prayed, "Father, if You've given him a new heart, and he doesn't need the defibrillator, tell me."

As she waited for an answer, a thought rose up within her, clear and strong. *Have another EKG. If the scar tissue is gone, you'll know.*

"We asked the doctor to do another EKG," Wanda says. "The doctor said he'd already done another one. There was no evidence of scar tissue."

That news came as no surprise to Craig. He knew his heart had been restored. He *knew* it with an assurance no one else could have. For while doctors and nurses, relatives and friends had been dealing with earthly matters, Craig had stepped over into a far more powerful realm.

"The last thing I remembered was sitting on the sofa that night reading my Bible, then...*I found myself walking down a road that was bright and beautiful. I could see the road for miles ahead of me.*

"Craig?" Wanda looked closely at her husband. He gasped three times then lay perfectly still, his face a horrible ashen color. "Craig, stop it or I'll call 911!"

There were rolling hills and meadows of the brightest green. Like new grass in spring. A fence made of hand-carved mahogany ran alongside the road.

My body shone with light, brightness. I noticed I didn't have on shoes. Someone walked beside me on my right.

Peace. I'd never known such peace.

The road led me into a cloud of white with beautiful, deep bronze-gold shimmering through it. The cloud surrounded me, encapsulating me and sustaining me. I felt suspended although only the cloud held me up.

The Lord spoke to me in my heart. He told me I'd been neglecting to do what He wanted me to do. He revealed myself to me, showing me my errors. He corrected me gently, with love I could feel.

Finally, I heard an audible voice that sounded like thunder say, "Go back. It's not your time."

Like batting an eye, I stepped out of the cloud. I appeared to be in a hospital room, although I couldn't imagine why I would be there. A tube down my throat kept me from talking, but I saw my family gathered around my bed. I couldn't stop looking around. Colors. I saw burgundy, purple, lavender, greens and reds. Colors I'd heard about all my life but never seen. I'd been colorblind since birth.

"When I could finally talk again, someone asked me how I felt," Craig recalls. "I said, 'I'm a new creature in Christ Jesus.' I was so new, I even had new eyesight. When the doctors told me I needed to have a defibrillator implanted, I felt like laughing. I didn't know a lot about hearts, but there were some things I did know. I knew for nine days I'd stood in the cloud of God's glory. What I needed, He had already given me."

Glory in the Grocery Store

"I checked out of the hospital against medical advice. They warned me of dire things to come and told me not to work for nine months. I'd been in the hospital for two weeks and lost 22 pounds. Still, I knew I was well. The thing I didn't know how to deal with was the depth of my desire to be back in that cloud."

The Lord helped Craig understand his experience by leading him to read about similar occurrences in the Bible. He read in Exodus about God appearing in a cloud, and about how Moses went *"into the midst of the cloud"* to meet with Him (Exodus 24:18). He read about the cloud that covered the mercy seat (Leviticus 16:2). He read in Acts 1:9 how *"a cloud received [Jesus] out of their sight."* Then he read that Jesus would come again in a cloud with power and glory (Luke 21:27).

When Craig went to the grocery store on his first day home from the hospital, an odd thing happened. Everyone stared at him. Finally, a Catholic priest tugged on his sleeve and asked, "What happened to you?"

Craig told him.

"I asked the Lord why people like the priest kept staring at me. He reminded me about when Moses came down from the mountain where he'd been in the presence of God. Moses had to put on a veil to cover the glory on his face. I didn't have to wear a veil, but it was that same glory that made people stare."

Craig St. Ledger returned to work a week after he left the hospital. He isn't the same man who died on January 19, 1994. Before, he was timid. Now, he is bold. Before, he was frustrated and angry. Now, he has peace. Before, God sometimes seemed distant. Now, he is constantly aware of God's omnipresence—*everywhere.*

"I studied the scripture about the glory cloud until I finally understood," Craig explains, "that the glory isn't far away. It's inside the heart of every Christian. *It's in me.*"

Before, Craig St. Ledger thought he was small bait in the spiritual kingdom. Now he knows that he is the temple of the Holy Spirit. That the very glory of God resides *in him* through the person of Jesus Christ.

The devil tried to kill Craig before he discovered the truth. But now it's too late. Craig St. Ledger knows who he is.

The devil knew all along.

Craig and Wanda have been Partners with Kenneth Copeland Ministries for 3 years!

Reaching Out for the Father's Hand

by Melanie Hemry

Marie Hill hummed to herself as she slipped on the X-ray gown and prepared for the ultrasound. Eight months pregnant with her fourth child, Marie stretched out on the table with a sigh.

Her doctor wanted to confirm her due date and make sure she wasn't going to give birth somewhere in a snowbank during their upcoming 2100-mile move across Canada. The airlines wouldn't let her fly this late in her pregnancy. So now, she faced a grueling trip across Canada in the middle of winter by car. Marie's mind raced ahead to the chore of sorting, packing and preparing for the move. She closed her eyes and relaxed during the ultrasound, grateful that her mother had arrived to help with the children.

When she opened her eyes again, Marie's mouth went dry at the sight before her. The ultrasound technician was crying. Turning her head, the technician tried to regain her composure. "Excuse me," she said, "we need to repeat your ultrasound on another machine." A few minutes later the woman returned with a doctor and moved Marie to a different ultrasound machine.

Fear gripped Marie's throat like a fist making it hard to swallow. She could feel her heartbeat pound against her temple in the tension-charged room. Finally, the second ultrasound was finished and Marie choked out two words.

"What's wrong?"

"I'll send this report to your obstetrician," the doctor answered. "All I can tell you is that your baby has eyes, a nose and a mouth."

Of course my baby has eyes, a nose and a mouth! Marie's mind screamed, *All babies have them. What is it that my baby* doesn't *have?*

"I was terrified," Marie admits. "I went home and told my husband, Gary, what the doctor had said. I was crying and filled with a nauseating sense of dread. It was such a horrible feeling that there was something wrong with my baby—something wrong inside of me.

"Gary was strong. He told me to get a grip on myself. Then he led me into the living room and put on a videotape of Kenneth Copeland. He made me listen to it so I could get my thoughts off the problem and onto the Word."

The following day Gary arrived at the obstetrician's office for a conference. Marie chose not to attend. She knew something was wrong, but she wasn't ready to hear the details. Gary, himself a physician with a specialty in emergency medicine, wasn't particularly worried. His wife's doctor was the best. He'd made sure of that.

Gary settled into the chair across from the obstetrician's desk and exchanged pleasantries for a few moments. "I'll let you look at the ultrasound for yourself," the obstetrician said, handing the films to Gary. Gary's trained eye scanned the picture. There, inside an 8-centimeter head, was a 5-centimeter cyst. His child did have eyes, a nose and a mouth.

She didn't have a brain.

"I'm sorry," the obstetrician said softly, "your baby has had an intrauterine stroke and the entire left hemisphere of the brain has been replaced with a cyst. You understand that where one major malformation exists, there are likely to be others. Under these circumstances, if you would like an abortion I can refer your wife to someone who will do it."

"We're Christians," Gary said, "we don't believe in abortion."

"I'm a Catholic and I don't believe in abortion either," the doctor said. "I suspected something was wrong because Marie has been small all along. The baby simply wasn't growing as it should. "I'll refer Marie to an obstetrical neurologist and..."

Gary interrupted, looking the other doctor squarely in the eye, "We both know that there is nothing any doctor anywhere can do for my baby. There is no medicine or surgery...nothing will help."

"That's right," the obstetrician admitted, looking away. "Your only hope is in God."

"My God has never let me down," Gary said, "and He's not going to do it now. I don't know how He'll get me out of this, but He will."

The obstetrician nodded. "I too believe in divine healing. And I believe we'll see more and more in the years to come. But if your baby isn't healed...."

One look from Gary stopped the other man's words. There was no room for "ifs" in this situation. Healing *had* to come. The alternative was unthinkable.

"What is it?" Marie asked when Gary arrived home looking pale and drawn.

"I can't tell you what it is," Gary said. "But it's bad."

"I went upstairs to our room and shut the door," Gary recalls. "I could still see the image of my baby's brainless head. I wanted to cry. I wanted to call my mother and tell her what a rotten deal life had dealt me.

"But I knew the only hope my baby had was my faith in God. So I pulled myself up by my ear and said, 'Listen, you've heard the Word of faith preached for 10 years. You know what to do, and now you *will* do it.' Then I raised my hands toward heaven. I said, 'You are Almighty God. You are my refuge and my fortress. You are my high tower. You are Jehovah Rapha. You are the healer of my family. You are the healer of my baby. There is none like You.'"

Twelve months earlier, Gary had made a New Year's resolution to spend time every day in prayer and in praise, meditating and reading the Scriptures. In the past three weeks, he had read the New Testament through three times.

Only one day before, the Lord had instructed Gary to go to a particular bookstore where He told him to buy two books. The books were *And Jesus Healed Them All* by Gloria Copeland, and *Healing the Sick* by T.L. Osborne. Gary could see a pattern now. The Lord had been prodding him, preparing him for the battle ahead.

But now it was time to fight the good fight of faith. Gary knew it wasn't something he could do part time or halfheartedly. He had to give it *all* his attention. Calling the hospital, he resigned from his job.

Gary Hill was reaching out for a miracle. Nothing else mattered.

Immediately, Gary began to hit Satan with the mightiest weapon in all of spiritual warfare. Praise. He spent literally hours praising God. He knew the Bible taught that God *inhabits* the praise of His people. But Gary had never experienced it like he did now.

"I was alone in my room," Gary remembers. "I'd been praising God for an hour or two when His presence came in like a cloud and knocked me flat. It was so overwhelming I tried to crawl out of the room. Then I thought, *What am I doing? I'm not going to leave God's presence.* So I lay still before Him. After half an hour His glory lifted.

"The next night, I'd been praising Him for an hour and a half and I felt like I was drunk in the Spirit. Suddenly I remembered a dream I'd had a few months before. In the dream a man brought his son to me. The boy was schizophrenic, had a brain tumor and I saw a suture line where he'd had brain surgery. In my dream I said, 'I'm going to lay my right hand on you and when I do, power from God will enter you and completely heal you.' I did as I said, and he was healed.

Gary interrupted, looking the other doctor squarely in the eye, "We both know that there is nothing any doctor anywhere can do for my baby. There is no medicine or surgery...nothing will help."

"Now, I saw a spiritual connection between that child's problem with his brain and my own child's problem. I knew the dream was a way of showing me what to do. I went to Marie. I said, 'I'm going to lay my right hand on your abdomen and when I do, the power of God is going to flow into our baby and completely heal it.' I did as I'd spoken...but nothing happened. I could tell that no power had been imparted.

"Then I laid my left hand on Marie's head. When I did, she fell under the power. While she lay there, I placed my right hand on her abdomen and the power of God went into the baby."

"I don't know how to explain what happened," Marie says. "It felt like the purity and love of God flowed into me and into the baby. For weeks after that, Gary and I would both wake up in the night with the sense of God around us like a cocoon. He seemed to hover over us. Fear was totally gone."

Gary continued to spend times of intense praise before the Lord each day. In addition, he saturated himself with the Word of faith. He listened to tapes of the Southwest Believers' Convention where Gloria Copeland taught on faith being in your heart and in your mouth. He watched the Copelands on television, watched videotapes from the Healing School and listened to cassette tapes. He read the New Testament through three more times.

"I had three pages of scriptures that Dodie Osteen had used to receive healing from cancer of the liver," Gary explains. "Three times a day, Marie and I each confessed those scriptures, personalizing them for our baby."

Gary meditated on Mark 11:23: *"Verily I say unto you, That whosoever shall say unto this mountain, Be thou removed, and be thou cast into the sea; and shall not doubt in his heart, but shall believe that those things which he saith shall come to pass; he shall have whatsoever he saith."*

It wasn't enough to believe. He had to speak to the mountain by confessing what he believed. His background in science taught him not to leave anything to chance.

How can I make sure I keep my faith confessions flowing? he wondered as he absently rolled the beads across his son's abacus. Suddenly he stopped and stared at the object in his hand.

An abacus. Used for counting. He set the abacus on the table before him and said, "With the stripes that wounded Jesus my baby was healed and made whole."

Then he moved one bead.

"With the stripes that wounded Jesus my baby was healed and made whole," he repeated and moved the second bead.

Gary repeated the confession until all 100 beads had been moved. Three times a day, Gary sat before the abacus, speaking his confessions. Once a day, he took the abacus to Marie and she made the same confession 100 times. Together, they confessed their child's healing 400 times a day.

Gary started doing the confessions as a simple act of obedience. But day after day, and week after week the words became so alive in his spirit that he *knew* his baby was whole. There was no room for doubt.

Marie's mother took over the care of their children and packed the house for the move so that Marie could spend time in the Word. The first week in January 1992, they began the drive across Canada. Once, 600 miles from the nearest hospital, Marie began having contractions, but the pains stopped and, miraculously, God held back the snow until they reached their destination.

"The closer we got to delivery," Gary recalls, "the more intense the attack from Satan. He bombarded our minds with thoughts of defeat and despair. But when I listened to my heart, I heard peace."

On January 16, 1992, Gary sat beside Marie in the labor room watching the fetal monitor. Occasionally a nurse would comment, "That's amazing! The contractions aren't even affecting the baby." Gary simply smiled at Marie and squeezed her hand. He had chosen not to tell the medical staff about the ultrasound report. The ultrasound was old news. Gary believed the report of the Lord.

Gary watched in wonder as his daughter, Carolyn, wiggled her way into the world that day. As he took her in his arms for the first time, joy exploded within him. This was the child for which he'd prayed, believed, and stood in faith. This was his seed. Blessed by Almighty God. It didn't take a medical degree to see that this child was perfect.

Intelligent eyes blinked at him from rosy-pink cheeks. Tiny hands wrapped themselves around Gary's finger in simple trust. Carolyn scored nine out of 10 on the Apgar infant assessment test. Great. No one could have ever guessed that just a month before, she'd had no brain...no natural hope...no future.

Today, Carolyn Hill is a bustling, busy, walking, talking 1-year-old. A delightful, radiantly happy little girl who still looks at her father with adoration and reaches for his hand in trusting confidence.

In that way, she is much like Gary Hill, himself. For he too knows what it's like to reach out to his Father and receive a miracle.

Update: Gary and Marie's little girl is now 3 1/2 years old. She plays "living books" on the computer, swims in the lake (with her lifejacket on), and builds toys out of Legos! Marie says she recently obtained a copy of the ultrasound and showed it to another radiologist. He too diagnosed the same problem...and then was very surprised to learn that Carolyn is normal. What an awesome God we serve!

Keeping the Promise in Sight

by Deena Farris

On a balmy evening in September 1981, Eugene De Paolo sat prayerfully on a secluded patch of lawn near the hotel where he was staying. Clutching his Bible in the darkness, he prayed—and waited for a word from God.

He had come to Albany, New York, to join the U.S. Air Force, to take the first step toward the dream that had been burning within him—the dream of learning to fly.

There was just one problem. His eyesight. As a toddler, Eugene had undergone surgery on both eyes to correct congenital amblyopia. Although his vision now was good, it was not perfect. And securing a pilot's slot in the U.S. Air Force required 20/20 vision. Without supernatural intervention, his flawed eyesight was irreversible. It would take a miracle, doctors agreed.

But then, Eugene believed in miracles. And he sensed his compelling desire to be a pilot had been placed within him for a reason greater than he could understand. To find that reason, he went straight to the source. "I wanted a word from the Lord," he said.

Sure enough, the word came. That night on the hotel lawn as Eugene searched the Scriptures and prayed in the Spirit, the Lord spoke.

Eugene, I will put you before kings and princes and those in high authority. You will wield the sword of the Word in Spirit and in Truth. Look not to the left, nor to the right for the enemy will try to divert you from the purposes that I am sending you to accomplish. For the Lord, your God, is raising you up to be a mighty warrior in the army of God.

"I didn't know what to think about such a message at the time," said Eugene. "But the Bible says God's sheep know His voice, and I knew those words were from the Lord."

The following morning, in obedience to the insistent prompting of the Spirit within him, Eugene De Paolo enlisted in the U.S. Air Force. "After I did it, I felt a great peace come over me," he recalled.

"For the next two years I felt like I was in a holding pattern. Following basic and technical training, I was assigned to the flight line at Eglin Air Force Base, [Florida] as a part of the maintenance crew."

Although he did not appear to be moving closer to his goal, Eugene kept it constantly in his sights. Prayerfully, he began to research the paths to pilot training. Then, in 1983, the Lord prompted Eugene to take action.

He filed a formal application for acceptance into the Air Force ROTC scholarship program. In response to his application, the scholarship board scheduled him to appear before them for a review. At last, the holding pattern was broken. It seemed Eugene was once again moving toward his dream.

Then, the forces of darkness unleashed an attack. The week of his review, Eugene's skin erupted in painful sores and boils. "The night before I was to meet the board, I just prostrated myself before the Lord and prayed," he said. "I knew if I missed this opportunity, it would be a year before I'd have another chance."

Despite the dark haze of pain that tried to cloud Eugene's thinking, the light of God's promise never flickered: *Look not to the left, nor to the right, for the enemy will try to divert you from the purposes that I am sending you to accomplish....*

The next morning Eugene stood before the review board, his body throbbing from the sores. For an excruciating hour, board members grilled him. Although it was tough, there was one very pleasant surprise. "When I arrived at the meeting, I discovered that the director of the board—the one in the position of giving the final recommendation for a pilot slot— was an elder in my church!"

Within hours after the completion of his board appearance, the sores that had plagued Eugene's body had disappeared entirely. The board unanimously recommended him for a scholarship. Satan had lost the first round.

"I just praised God," Eugene remembered. "Even though the scholarship was for a navigator slot, rather than a pilot slot, I felt like my foot was in the door."

Before he even had a chance to report for classes in January, however, that door began to close. The call came from the director of the education office. "Eugene," he began, "I am sorry to inform you that the Air Force will not be able to qualify you for the navigator slot in the ROTC program."

They had reviewed his medical records. Eugene's history of eye problems disqualified him. As an alternative, they offered him a slot in a technical capacity. Eugene accepted.

"I'm sure God allowed Satan to take away the first scholarship so that I could continue to believe Him for the best," said Eugene. "He told me I would fly as a pilot, not a navigator. So I continued to stand on His Word."

The next three years were a frenzied blur of academic activity, punctuated by repeated eye exams. Time after time he read the eye chart. Time after time he failed the exam. His eyesight remained unchanged.

Eugene needed something to boost his faith. That something came in the form of faith tapes by Kenneth and Gloria Copeland.

Eugene was so encouraged by the Copelands' teachings that in 1986, he painstakingly assembled a model of a Lear jet and mailed it to their ministry headquarters. He included a letter relating God's promise to him and his subsequent struggles and prayers.

Within days Kenneth Copeland contacted Eugene, thanking him for the model. "I set myself in agreement with you for a perfect medical record with approval needed to receive the pilot slot," he wrote.

As the months passed, the number of prayer warriors praying on Eugene's behalf began to mount: KCM, Eugene's college roommates, his family, his church.... A college professor and a group of elders approached Eugene at separate times. Though each one knew of Eugene's desire to fly, they knew nothing about the prophecy he had been given five years earlier. Each bore the same message: "Eugene, the Lord is raising you up to be a mighty warrior. He will set you before kings and princes and those in high authority."

Still, with only one year of college remaining and no pilot slot in sight, it seemed Eugene's dreams of flying were about to crash and burn. "Things were looking pretty hopeless," he admitted.

Then the light of God's promise once again broke through. "I was in the car, driving from Orlando, [Florida] to Daytona Beach, [Florida]," Eugene recalled. "I had just plugged in a tape by Kenneth Copeland and was listening to him describe an experience he had when he was learning to fly a multi-engine aircraft. He talked about how the instructor tried to overwhelm him in mid-flight to test his ability to handle crises."

Eugene was familiar with the technique. A good pilot must learn to be faithful to do what he's been trained to do, even when emergencies arise around him. Suddenly Eugene understood what was happening. Satan was trying to overwhelm him. If Eugene was going to fly he would have to act faithfully on the Word.

At that moment, the sky filled with color and two great rainbows curved and shimmered across the watery gray horizon. Eugene watched them in awe.

"I knew the rainbow was a symbol of God's promise," he says. "I also knew that God is not the author of destruction. He would not destroy the plan for my life which He had so carefully set in motion. But, *two* rainbows?"

Eugene remembered God's special promises to him. God had given him two promises—the written Word and a personal promise spoken directly to his heart. Those two promises together would see him through.

Minutes later, Eugene glanced up at a sign on the side of the road. It read "Columbus A.F.B. 1 Mile." Not unusual—except that Columbus Air Force Base is in Mississippi—and Eugene was in Florida. What could that mean?

When Eugene got back to college he looked up Columbus Air Force Base in his ROTC material. There he found what he had already suspected—it was a pilot training base. God was clearly telling Eugene not to give up. He was telling him to stand, and stand, and keep standing on the promises he had been given.

On October 1, 1987, Eugene reported for his commissioning physical. It was the last one allowed. The one that would determine his Air Force career.

Eugene spent the night before the physical praying. And at precisely 9 a.m. he began his final eye exam. "E...A...P...Q..." On and on he read, calling out the letters with perfect accuracy. Eugene's eyesight was checked and rechecked. No one could believe it. The stunned examiners stared at Eugene. His eyesight was perfect.

Enraged, the devil launched a final, feeble attack. Eugene's blood test now indicated an unacceptable cholesterol level. Unwilling to let anything overwhelm him now, Eugene was retested. The results were normal. Eugene was given a clean bill of health.

"The last attack against my perfect medical record was against the blood," he said. "Doesn't the devil know he is defeated when it comes to blood? The blood of Jesus prevails all the time!"

On April 6, 1989, Eugene De Paolo graduated as a pilot in the U.S. Air Force. His assignment? To fly the C-21 Lear jet.

"The mission of a Lear jet," he explains, "is to transport *those in high authority.*"

And that is exactly what Eugene does. During Operation Desert Storm, Eugene was assigned to transport many commanding officials including Army Gen. Norman Schwarzkopf.

Today, Eugene does indeed *wield the sword of the Word in Spirit and in Truth.* He has had the opportunity to witness to such notables as American Red Cross President Elizabeth Dole and Sen. Edward Kennedy. Always, he prays for those the Lord entrusts to his flying expertise. And no matter what crises arise around him, he is still faithfully keeping God's promises in sight.

Update: Eugene continues to serve in the United States Air Force. He has flown all over the world in support of every military operation during the last three years, and currently flies the largest aircraft in the U.S. inventory—the C-5 Galaxy. In 1995, Eugene married the former Kay Sylvester. Together they serve in their local church in the music ministry.

Eugene has been a Partner with Kenneth Copeland Ministries for 11 years!

My God
Can Turn It Around!

by Melanie Hemry

Jo Anne Murray stepped out of the neurologist's office gripping a piece of paper listing all the tests she would undergo in the next two weeks. People stared as she lurched to the right, falling against the wall of the corridor.

The long hall seemed to spin and flip as she groped for balance. Her right arm shook uncontrollably as she reached out to steady herself. Tentatively, she took another step, but this time her right leg gave way and she tumbled against the wall again.

Brain tumor...multiple sclerosis...brain tumor...multiple sclerosis. The doctor's words echoed in her mind. *Your symptoms indicate one or the other.*

As Jo Anne tottered to her car, questions clamored within her—each demanding an answer.

What if I have a brain tumor? They would cut it out. *What if it was malignant?* I'd die.

What is multiple sclerosis? I don't know. *Could multiple sclerosis be worse than a brain tumor?* I don't know! *What will happen to my son?* I don't know! *Should I tell Mom?* I don't know!

"JUST LEAVE ME ALONE!" Jo Anne cried, leaning her head on the steering wheel. There was nothing she could do about it all anyway. Nothing but wait....

Two weeks later, Jo Anne was back in the doctor's office. Rubbing sweaty palms against her skirt, she wondered about the results of her tests. Initially, she had hoped the diagnosis would be multiple sclerosis instead of a brain tumor. But when she had read about multiple sclerosis, she'd changed her mind. The list of symptoms seemed endless.

Skipping over the medical jargon, she'd scanned the pages of the books in the hospital medical library for a description of the treatment. Even now the words she had seen there jarred her. *No cure.*

The muscles of MS patients gradually quit working because of a malfunction in the brain. Eventually, victims become helpless cripples. The blessed ones, Jo Anne decided, were the ones whose minds were destroyed along with the muscles.

Brain tumor or multiple sclerosis. Jo Anne drew a shuddering breath as the doctor opened the exam room door. *Heads...I lose. Tails...I lose.*

"You don't have a brain tumor," the doctor said, reading through Jo Anne's chart. As he continued, the room began to spin. Jo Anne heard fragments of his words as if from a distance.

"...Abnormal EEG...improper stimulus...right arm and leg...multiple sclerosis...give you phenobarbital for the seizures...Jo Anne, do you have any questions?"

No. Jo Anne had no questions. Instead, horrifying images crowded her mind.

She remembered vividly a new patient she had seen at the hospital where she worked in X-ray. He'd been in a wheelchair designed especially for him. His arms were tied to arm rests. His legs were tied to leg rests. He was tied across the chest to keep him from falling forward. He wore a band across his forehead that was tied to the back of the chair. He was 35 years old.

He had multiple sclerosis, Jo Anne thought. *Now I do too.*

"Somehow I made it to my car before the screaming and sobbing began. It didn't seem real. I always thought the good guys would win in life. I couldn't think of anything I'd ever done that was bad enough to deserve this.

"I screamed at God. This only confirmed what I'd thought about Him all along. I had been raised in church, but all I saw there was hypocrisy. I'd decided long ago to be independent. I hadn't needed or wanted God and church before. I certainly didn't want Him now—or at least I thought so."

Months passed and Jo Anne continued her lonely war against the chilling symptoms of MS. As the disease progressed, so did her emotional reactions to it. First, she was afraid. Then grief-stricken. Finally, anger took over.

Nights were endless hours of sleeplessness. Fatigue sapped what little strength she had for her job and her 10-year-old son Joe.

Simple tasks became a chore. With increasing frequency Jo Anne found herself unable to lift or grip with her right hand. Reaching for something on her dresser one day, her trembling arm knocked over a bottle of perfume and hand lotion.

The anger that had simmered inside her for months erupted. Grabbing the perfume bottle, she threw it into the hall where it shattered. Hand lotion followed, then books, pens, folders, writing tablets—everything within Jo Anne's reach flew against the wall.

Standing in the hallway, Jo Anne glared at the mess and then addressed the Lord.

"God," she said, sarcasm dripping from each word, "I'd like to personally thank You for what You've done for me! But in the future, when You're looking for someone to bless, please don't look for me...I pass!" Then she slid down the lotion-spattered wall and sobbed.

Two months later, Jo Anne asked her doctor what would happen if she stopped taking the phenobarbital. Sensing her anger, the doctor allowed her to try it and see.

Ten days after Jo Anne stopped taking the drug, she began drifting into walls, unable to walk. The depression worsened and her symptoms intensified until she finally returned to the medication.

"For eight long months," Jo Anne says, "I alternated between anger and depression. Then the pain started. It began as a nagging backache. I had a ruptured disc years before, so I assumed this was a flare-up of the old injury. The pain became intolerable and I went back to the doctor. She told me to take time off and rest, because the pain was related to multiple sclerosis. I refused. Instead, I drove my son to Florida for a vacation."

By the time she returned from Florida, the pain had become devastating. It felt like a knife twisting in her back every time she moved. Limping into the doctor's office, Jo Anne hung her head and cried. Yes, she agreed, she was ready to be admitted to the hospital.

The next few weeks were a haze of pain. Groggy from pain medication, Jo Anne flipped through the television channels trying to focus her eyes on the screen. Recognizing Richard Roberts, she started to change the channel. But something stopped her. His eyes. *His eyes were smiling.* Fading into a drugged sleep, Jo Anne heard these words, "No matter what your situation, my God can turn it around!"

Later, Jo Anne roused and glanced at the television screen again. This time she saw a preacher dressed—oddly enough—in blue jeans. *His eyes were smiling too!* Drifting off to sleep again she heard him say, "I'm Kenneth Copeland, and remember, Jesus *is* Lord!"

For the next few days Jo Anne drifted in and out of sleep and caught bits and pieces from the television. Once she awoke to see Richard Roberts pointing at her. Jo Anne pointed at herself and said, "Me?"

"Yes," Richard answered through the television screen, "you in the hospital with back pain."

Don't you think that out of thousands of people that are watching this, there would be at least one person in the hospital with back pain? snapped a cynical inner voice.

"Yeah," Jo Anne countered, "...Me!"

"...I want you to get out of bed," Richard continued, "and put your hand on the TV screen."

You're being foolish, the inner cynic argued desperately. *This is ridiculous! What is touching a TV screen going to do for you?*

Jo Anne swung her legs off the bed and staggered to the television. She couldn't reach it! "If you can't reach it," Richard continued, "just reach your hand toward mine!"

"This is eerie," Jo Anne said, lifting her hand toward his. Following his prayer, she crawled back into bed and drifted into a restless sleep.

"Later that day," Jo Anne explains, "I got out of bed again. I knelt beside the bed and said, 'God, I don't know if You're there...and I don't know if You can hear me, but if You're there, and if You can hear me...I need help!'

"Back in bed, I wondered if He heard me. My body certainly didn't feel any different. I didn't look any different. But that very day, something changed. A sweet, precious longing was born inside me! It was a longing for God. Suddenly, I wanted to know Him! And I knew I wasn't alone anymore."

Even through a haze of pain and drugs, Jo Anne's desire for God continued to grow. When she wasn't sleeping, she was watching, listening and learning from KVTN, Channel 25, the local Christian television station.

The God she heard about from there was love! He was peace! He was kindness! He was everything beautiful that any poet could write. He was absolutely everything Jo Anne had been looking for all her life.

For the remainder of her 14-day hospital stay, Jo Anne listened to Kenneth and Gloria Copeland and others talk about healing. Could they be right? Could it be that God hadn't done this to her? That He desired to heal her?

Two days after she was discharged from the hospital Jo Anne stopped taking her medication. A few days later she began to tilt to the right, bumping into things. Defeated, and tired of fighting, Jo Anne went back on the phenobarbital and swore she'd never try to get off again.

"Still," Jo Anne remembers, "that desire to know Him continued to grow in me. Then, a friend of my mother's loaned me a hundred tapes by Kenneth and Gloria Copeland. I listened hungrily to every one of them. Finally...finally, I began to understand what God was telling me. Healing was mine, simply because I was His!

"...finally, I began to understand what God was telling me. Healing was mine, simply because I was His!"

"I looked up healing scriptures and prayed them over and over. I hung onto Isaiah 53:5, Matthew 8:17 and 1 Peter 2:24 with all my might—day after day, week after week and month after month."

In August of 1989, Jo Anne traveled to Fort Worth, Texas, for Kenneth Copeland Ministries' Southwest Believers' Convention. It wasn't healing that Jo Anne sought at that convention—it was the Healer. She found Him in a new and powerful way through the Baptism in the Holy Spirit.

Even though Jo Anne never stood in a healing line, she gradually sensed in her spirit that she had been healed. She had been taking two 60-milligram tablets of phenobarbital a day for over a year. Twice she'd tried to quit—twice she'd gotten worse. Still, her heart told her to try again.

"My natural mind had a fit," Jo Anne says. "It told me I was just asking to be hurt again! It reminded me of my other failures, and asked why I thought anything was different now.

"I told my mind that by Jesus' stripes I'd been healed. I read Scripture to my mind and preached to my mind. And I stopped taking the phenobarbital." This time it was for good.

It's been over three years since Jo Anne Murray was healed of multiple sclerosis—a disease with "no cure." She doesn't tilt to the right anymore. She doesn't bump into things. Rooms and walls don't flip around anymore. Her right arm and hand are strong.

As an instructor at the school of Radiologic Technology at Jefferson Regional Medical Center, a single parent and an active member of Victory Christian Fellowship church, Jo Anne's busy lifestyle is a constant testimony of God's healing power. And her son is so enthusiastic about her miraculous recovery that he has encouraged her to write her story and share it with as many people as possible.

"There are so many people who are hurting,"

Jo Anne says. "They are in physical, mental and emotional pain, simply because they don't know what God has done for them. They are the reason I keep telling my story. The Lord wants them to see that healing has been provided for them. It's theirs! It's a gift that's been bought and paid for! All they have to do is receive it!"

Hardly a day goes by now when Jo Anne doesn't think about that gift. "There are times," she says, "when I'm walking somewhere that I'll be so overwhelmed with joy that I just want to take off and run!" And, amazingly enough, that's exactly what she does.

Update: When KCM asked Jo Anne if she had continued to experience freedom from MS since this article was first published, she answered us with an emphatic, "MOST DEFINITELY!" As a reference to time, Jo Anne told us that her son was only 10 years old when she was healed. Today he is 17. Her concluding statement was, "God is not enough—He's too much!"

Jo Anne has been a Partner with Kenneth Copeland Ministries for 7 years!

Tiny Warrior

by Gina Jennings

"Guardian angels are watchin' over me,
Making sure that the Father's Word
Is carried out for me.
Watchin' over me while I sleep,
They protect me when I play.
Guardian angels are watchin' over me."

My mercy hovers over your boy, the words rang clearly in Carin Prickett's mind. They'd caught her attention just a few days ago as she'd listened to one of Gloria Copeland's teaching tapes. She'd known they were important even then. But now she knew they were crucial.

Looking down at her 2$^{1}/_{2}$-year-old son, Jonathan, lying limp in her lap, his eyes glazed, fighting to stay conscious, Carin let the phrase wash over her mind again. *My mercy hovers over your boy.* She could almost hear Gloria's voice. "God gave that word to me for my son. Now you take it and receive it for your children too...." [1]

Jonathan's eyes rolled backward for a moment as he slipped toward unconsciousness. The movement of the car as it rushed toward Bethany General Hospital jostled his small, seemingly lifeless limbs. Beside him, his dad, Dr. Josh Prickett, gripped the steering wheel, pressed the accelerator toward the floor, and continued to pray in the Spirit.

He knew the seriousness of the situation. Just moments before, he had seen his son topple face first from a shopping cart onto the cement floor of the store where he and Carin had been shopping. He'd heard the crack of his neck. And, being a physician, he'd recognized the danger signs immediately.

"Jonathan, can you move your hands?" Carin asked for the 20th time as they tore through the Oklahoma City traffic.

"No," Jonathan whispered weakly.

"Can you move your feet?"

"No..."

Cradling Jonathan's tiny motionless form in her arms, Carin knew that the mother's heart within her should be racing in panic, beating out a rhythm of terror against her chest. That would, after all, be the "natural" reaction. But instead, she had been quieted by a supernatural peace. "It was like God just said, 'It's going to be all right,'" she recalls.

Several years before, such an assurance from God might have been difficult—perhaps even impossible—for Carin to believe. "I had gone through some very rough times," she explains. "I felt as though God had totally abandoned me and there was no hope for my life. Then I started listening to Kenneth Copeland on television. He'd talk about victory and I'd think, *I'm not walking in victory and I've had Jesus in my heart for years.*

"At that point I started buying up every tape, every book, anything of the Copelands I could get hold of. I'd listen to them over and over again."

It had been more than six years since she'd first heard the Copelands, yet now as Carin sped toward the emergency room with her injured son, she was still listening. Not only to the voices of the Copelands, but much more importantly, to the comforting voice of the Holy Spirit Himself.

At the hospital, reports were ominous. Jonathan's arms and legs were still showing no signs of feeling. X-rays revealed a blockage in the airway within his neck and a fracture to his skull.

As Jonathan continued to teeter on the edge of unconsciousness, Josh and Carin continued to pray. "Other members of God's army joined in prayer with us," says Carin. "And when a second set of X-rays was taken, the blockage to the airway was completely gone."

It was an odd and somewhat encouraging development. Yet serious dangers remained. "The skull fracture was still there, so we just kept praying and refused to be moved by what we saw."

Because the severity of the injury to Jonathan's skull indicated possible brain damage, a CT scan was scheduled. As the Pricketts waited for the scan, the minutes ticked slowly by. "I was holding Jonathan, and we would lay him down on the bed every few minutes," Carin recalls. "His eyes were still glassed over and rolling back in his head like he was going to pass out. We couldn't get him to do anything. We couldn't get him to look up or say anything."

Both Carin and Josh knew, however, that Jonathan, even at 2½ years old, was more than just a helpless toddler. He was a "faith-kid" who not long before had proudly announced he was "a warrior in God's army!" And his parents had been faithfully planting the Word of God in his heart almost since birth.

"We always pray with him at night before he goes to bed. Then we put on Kellie Copeland's album and let her sing him to sleep with the Word," says Carin. "Albums like Kellie's have an effect on kids' faith. I really believe it's one of the most incredible ways to plant good seed."

The Pricketts knew there was plenty of that good seed inside Jonathan. So, no matter how still and silent their tiny warrior lay, their faith remained unshaken. "We knew in our knower what the outcome would be," says Carin. "It was just an opportunity to watch God be God."

Outside the hospital, the afternoon sun dimmed and dusk began to curl its way across the sky. Inside, nothing changed. The fluorescent lights of the emergency room shone white and cold on Jonathan's skin. And his parents simply watched and prayed.

It was the bright sound of Jonathan's voice that startled them from their quiet vigil.

"Mom!" he said, springing suddenly into eager motion. "I want a drink!" Then, sitting up, he began to sing from the album his mother had so often played for him...

> *"Guardian angels are watchin' over me,*
> *Making sure that the Father's Word*
> *Is carried out for me.*
> *Watchin' over me while I sleep,*
> *They protect me when I play.*
> *Guardian angels are watchin' over me."* [2]

The change was so instantaneous, so dramatic that "it was just like day and night!" says Carin.

"Can you move your hands?" she asked joyfully.

"Yeah!"

As if to demonstrate, Jonathan jumped from the bed. "Within seconds after that, he was playing with the equipment in the emergency room as if nothing had ever happened."

The CT scan was taken as scheduled, and when the radiologist examined the results, he found that the fracture which had been so clearly revealed by the previous X-rays had disappeared.

"Judging by the type of injury indicated on the X-ray, there should have been some bleeding on the brain and some layer damage. But the CT scan didn't even show a fracture. The radiologist couldn't explain it," Carin says with a grin, "but we can!"

Jonathan was released from the hospital that night. The abrasions on his head were already fading. And though his neck was somewhat sore, his faith was in fine form. In fact, when his mother explained that the soreness might persist for a while, his response was quick and sure.

"No it won't! I'm just fine," he said.

Carin smiles today as she remembers that moment—and she knows with every beat of her mother's heart that he is absolutely right.

Update: Today Jonathan remains perfectly normal... as if nothing ever happened.

Footnotes:
[1] *Fruit of the Spirit,* cassette series by Gloria Copeland.
[2] "Guardian Angels" from *Precious Moments* by Kellie Copeland Kutz. Written by Bill and Dyan Deaton.

Josh and Carin have been Partners with Kenneth Copeland Ministries for 13 years!

The Miraculous "Mending" of Jessica Salvage

by Melanie Hemry

On June 2, 1989, Susan Salvage paced the waiting room of a children's hospital in Pennsylvania. In a few minutes she would finally have answers to the questions that had plagued her for months.

Susan glanced at her tiny daughter, Jessica, asleep in her arms. At 10 months, Jessica barely tipped the scales at 10 pounds.

Susan had known from the beginning that something was wrong with Jessica. And it *wasn't* just the imaginations of a nervous new mother as so many had suggested. Jessica had been born with a horrified expression on her face and wild jerky movements.

When it was clear that she had no sucking reflex, doctors said she was "a little lazy." As a nurse, Susan knew that sucking was a neurological reflex—and its absence indicated a neurological problem. *But what?* And what caused the chronic vomiting and weight loss? Why at 8 months had Jessica's muscle tone been so poor that she couldn't even hold up her head?

A nurse summoned Susan into Jessica's hospital room where a group of doctors—specialists in various fields of pediatric medicine—waited. Finally, after months of testing, Susan would have answers to her questions.

"The result of the MRI was definitive," the pediatric neurologist began. "Jessica has Agenesis of the Corpus Callosum with immature white matter."

Susan tried to ask a question, but suddenly her mouth was dry. She wiped clammy hands on her skirt and tried to focus her attention on the doctor's words. They were gently—very gently—trying to explain the diagnosis. *Agenesis of the Corpus Callosum.* Susan understood only too well what it meant. Her daughter had been born with part of her brain missing.

"You are already aware of Jessica's gastroesophageal reflux," the doctor said, "but there is more. She has hypotonia—poor muscle tone, a kidney syndrome known as Cystinuria, and essentially no immune system to fight off infection. Do you have any questions?"

"Will Jessica learn to walk?" Susan asked.

"No...we don't think so."

"Will she sit up?"

"No...we don't think so."

"Will she learn to talk?"

"No...we don't think so."

"What will Jessica be able to do?"

"We don't know."

"Are you telling me that she won't do *anything?*"

"Well, there are some fine institutions...."

Susan's hand flew to her protruding abdomen. "I'm eight months pregnant!" she cried. "What about *this* baby?"

"We don't know...."

Susan stumbled from the conference room. She had her answers now. It had simply never occurred to her that there wouldn't be a solution. Pressing Jessica against her heaving chest, Susan walked out of the hospital.

Her nightmare wasn't over.

It had just begun.

"I'd made a decision to live for the Lord back in 1978," Susan says. "I kept that commitment for three weeks before I turned my back on Him. Now, faced with the horrible reality of my child's condition, I had nowhere to turn.

"I was furious with God," Susan admits. "I'd been furious with Him since my mother died when I was 15. Now this. It was too much. I'd been brought up with the mistaken idea that God gives and God takes away—and it seemed He'd done more taking than giving to me."

On July 15, 1989, Susan and Patrick Salvage's second daughter, Kimberly was born. They watched anxiously for the familiar symptoms they'd seen in Jessica—jerky movements, sleeplessness and a high-pitched, pitiful cry that sounded more like a sparrow than a child. They did not manifest. Kimberly, it seemed, had been born healthy.

"Back home, we tried to pick up the pieces of our lives," Susan explains. "Medical expenses already had our finances in shambles. Patrick was working 70 hours a week and going to school at the same time. He was desperately trying to find a way to support our family and pay staggering amounts of medical expenses.

"I was trying to find a way to get through each day. I fed Kimberly three times each night and it seemed Jessica never slept. She screamed for hours while I walked her and tried everything I knew to help her."

Help came from unexpected sources. Patrick's cousin, Nancy Marie, a Spirit-filled Christian, began encouraging Patrick and Susan by telling them about the power of God. A single parent with four children, she made time to help Susan with the babies. Meanwhile Diane, a friend they met through Nancy Marie, stood in the gap as an intercessor, praying for the family daily and explaining the Word to them.

In answer to her prayer, God sent Brenda, a born-again, occupational therapist, to work with Jessica. Brenda began telling Susan about God's healing power, and she, too, began praying for the family. One day Brenda recognized that Susan was being stretched too far and was physically and emotionally exhausted. "Susan," she advised, flipping on the television, "try watching the Copelands."

"I did start watching Kenneth and Gloria Copeland on television," Susan recalls. "They talked about a God I didn't know. One Who didn't kill, or make people sick, but rather a God Who healed and made people whole. I listened because they spoke hope to me. I knew in my mind that God was the way to go, but my faith was still in the medical profession."

One Saturday morning in November 1989, exhaustion, depression and despair took their toll on Susan's mind. Minutes and hours, days and nights, weeks and months of sleeplessness and stress blurred together into nothingness. "I went downstairs to start the laundry," Susan says, "and I couldn't remember what to do. I sat on the stairs and cried. I didn't know if I'd given Jessica her medicine, or measured Kimberly's formula. I couldn't function, and it felt like I was losing my mind.

"I kept saying over and over, 'I know my name is Susan Salvage.'" That was the only thing she knew for sure. There on the basement stairs, Susan cried out to God.

"Lord," she said, "I know I'm rotten and I've been straddling the fence, but if You're up there...help me!"

"Suddenly it felt like something warm wrapped around my head, and I felt something snap and lift off of me. I was enveloped in peace, and I seemed to hear these words, *Just put one foot forward.*"

Susan made it through the next few months exactly as the Lord had told her: one step at a time. In December, Jessica was admitted to the hospital emergency room 17 times. In January she was rushed to the emergency room 14 times.

Month after month passed as Patrick, Susan, doctors and nurses fought for Jessica's life. Her immune system was so weak that a simple infection which began in her ear quickly spread through her entire body. Susan saturated herself in the Word and in faith daily. She prayed for Jessica's healing and confessed it to anyone who would listen.

On July 13, 1990, Jessica had a seizure and reached the emergency room with a temperature registered at 106.8 degrees. She was unconscious. "I gave up," Susan says. "That night I stopped living for Jessica and put her in God's arms. I asked the Lord if it was His will to take her home and He answered a resounding, NO!

"I jumped up and commanded the devil to take his hands off my child in Jesus' Name. I shouted that she had been healed 2,000 years ago and that I wouldn't accept anything less. At 2:30 that morning she sat up and wanted to eat. By 5 a.m. we took her home."

> **Gloria looked deeply into Susan's eyes. "The Bible says that He sent His Word and healed them," she said. "This child's sickness doesn't glorify God. This child *healed* glorifies God."**

In October 1990, Brenda invited Patrick and Susan to attend a meeting in Teaneck, New Jersey, where Kenneth and Gloria Copeland were preaching. The couple eagerly accepted. At the conclusion of Saturday's Healing School, Gloria called for those who wanted to receive prayer for healing. Susan was ready. She swept Jessica into her arms and headed toward the front of the auditorium.

Susan waited patiently as Gloria laid hands on one person after another. Then, at last, her moment came. Pausing, Gloria looked deeply into Susan's eyes. "The Bible says that He sent His Word and healed them," she said. "This child's sickness doesn't glorify God. This child *healed* glorifies God. Don't let anyone tell you any different."

At that moment, something within Susan changed. "Once and for all I stopped blaming God," she says. "I started playing scripture tapes over Jessica and the scripture started speaking to me."

The battle wasn't over. More than a year would pass before the physical changes would come. But a power had been released in both Susan and in Jessica that would not stop working until the victory was theirs.

In late October 1990, Patrick and Susan were told that Jessica needed surgery. "It was such a blow," Susan recalls, "I'd been telling everyone that Jessica was healed by Jesus' stripes. Now *this*. I was driving home from the doctor's office crying.

"'Father,' I prayed, 'What's going on? I look like a fool. I've told everyone that Jessica is healed. I don't know what to think!'

"I glanced up at the arches over McDonald's as I spoke and suddenly I wasn't in my car. I wasn't even in my city....

"I was standing at the bottom of a cement block. I saw a man strapped with His arms stretched out. I could only see His back—but He looked half dead. A soldier standing behind Him cracked a whip. It ripped the flesh on the man's back down to the bone. The sight

was so horrifying I felt sick and turned my face away. As I turned, I felt something hot and wet on my face. I rubbed it off, then looked at my hand. It was blood.

"An instant later, I was back in my car driving past McDonald's, sobbing. The Lord spoke to me and said, *That was the stripe He took for Jessica. Now believe it. She is healed!*"

Susan Salvage never doubted again...she had seen the stripe.

One year later, in October 1991, Susan said the words she'd spoken thousands of times, "Come on Jessica, walk to Mommy." This time Jessica slid off the sofa and took one tiny step...then fell.

"I knelt in front of her," Susan says, "and said, 'Jessica, just say by Jesus' stripes I can do it.'"

Jessica pulled herself up again. "She turned to me and took a step," Susan explains, "then two steps... three...four...five.... I backed away on my knees. Six... seven...eight...nine...ten...eleven...twelve...she fell, then pulled herself up and walked right into my arms."

Each time Jessica took a step, Susan watched in awe. "The amazing thing about Jessica's learning to walk," Susan says, "is that the neurological pathway necessary to send the signal from her brain didn't exist. Every time she lifted her leg and took a step, I wondered, *How?*"

A note from one of Jessica's medical records, written by one of her neurologists, reads: "When one looks over the early records it is apparent that Jessica has come a long way and done better than anyone imagined. We are simply not sure what caused this."

Susan and Patrick Salvage are *very* sure what caused the change. It was the power of God Himself.

God has brought about many other changes in Susan

and Patrick's lives as well. For example, they asked Him to surround them with a praying, faith-filled church. And that's exactly what He did. A career change for Patrick moved them from Pennsylvania to Orlando, Fla., where they have found a wonderful church.

Yet even with many answers to prayer, Susan had a question. "I asked the Lord why Jessica didn't get an instant miracle," Susan says. "I wondered why when Gloria laid hands on her she didn't get down and walk over and say 'Hi everybody!'

"He told me to read John 4:49-53. A man had asked Jesus to heal his son. Later he asked his servants when the boy had begun to *amend.* I knew instantly—that's what happened to Jessica. A mending." Day by day, step by step, Jessica is mending still.

Small things mark the progress of her miracle. For example, recently when the house became too quiet, Susan started looking for Jessica. "She had pulled a chair into the bathroom, moved it next to the sink, climbed onto it, and was brushing her teeth!" Susan says, laughing.

Today, Jessica Salvage is a busy little 4-year-old who beams from under a halo of curls. She walks, but more often runs. She brushes her teeth, opens doors and is beginning to talk.

Jessica's favorite pastime is singing songs about Jesus. And why not? It is, after all, because of the stripe He bore for her that she is able to sing at all.

Update: Today Jessica is 7 years old. In April of 1994, she and her family attended the Tallahassee Victory Campaign in Tallahassee, Florida. Gloria prayed for the healing of her eyes.

Because of her eyesight, she is considered 100 percent

handicapped. In May of '94, Jessica's ophthalmologists tested her eyes and said she no longer needs glasses! She is also talking more in sentences and continuing to improve at a miraculous rate.

Her case nurse recently said, "Now this little girl Jessica has done better than anyone expected. She is a miracle..."

Pat and Susan have been Partners with Kenneth Copeland Ministries for 6 years!

Race for a Miracle

by Melanie Hemry

Rich Sprenkel slid behind the wheel of his Jeep and started the engine. He knew better. He knew better than to drive when he'd been drinking, and he knew better how to live than the way he'd been living.

Rich had been raised in a Christian home where values were taught from the Bible. But somewhere a seed of rebellion had taken root. Now, at 19, Rich partied and drank with his college friends, disregarding his father's warnings.

Rich backed the car out of its parking space. *I'll go slow,* he reasoned, pulling onto Main Street in Chico, California. And he did drive slow. Slow enough to see the dog that darted into the street. Slow enough to swerve and miss hitting it. But somehow not slow enough to keep the Jeep from flipping over throwing Rich and all three of the friends with him out of the wreckage.

Rich's head hit the curb with a sickening snap, breaking his neck in four places. His skull was fractured from his right ear to the top of his head.

The unforgiving cement ripped off half of his ear. As though determined to finish the job, the Jeep rolled two more times and landed on him. The impact broke Rich's pelvis in four places. A piece of metal from the top pierced his side, protruding halfway through his stomach.

Rich Sprenkel's battered body gave up. On that cruel April night in 1984, crumpled under the weight of the Jeep, he simply quit breathing.

A man living nearby heard the crash and immediately ran to the scene. Kneeling beside Rich's lifeless form, he began CPR. Later that night, Rich's parents, Rich Sr. and Elaine Sprenkel, waited outside the emergency room of Enloe Memorial Hospital for news of their son's condition.

"Your son's spinal cord is severed in two places," the doctor explained, "he won't make it through the night."

The Sprenkels knew that by medical standards, the doctor spoke the truth. They had rushed into the emergency room where Rich was being treated only minutes after he arrived. They had witnessed the gruesome scene that no parent should see, and they knew that Rich's injuries had taken him beyond the reach of mere medical technology. The only way Rich would make it through the night was by the intervention of Almighty God.

And they planned to see that he got it.

"I prayed in tongues over my son in that emergency room," Rich's father recalls. "Then we prayed for divine intervention. We asked for Rich's healing based on 1 Peter 2:24. I knew healing belonged to us, and at some level in his spirit, Rich knew it, too. We'd taken him to his first Believers' Convention to hear Kenneth Copeland preach when he was 12 years old. He had heard the Word."

News of Rich's injuries blazed through the Pleasant Valley Assembly of God Church as members initiated the prayer chain. Far more than the typical single-church prayer chain, this string of prayer warriors included more than the Pleasant Valley members, more than the Assembly of God churches in Chico. It reached through every church in Chico, California.

Full Gospel, Independent, Methodist, and Baptist churches began to pray. Presbyterians and Episcopalians, Catholics and Lutherans—all united in prayer.

Hour after agonizing hour passed that night as Rich's parents paced the waiting area outside surgery. "How many times did I tell him he was living wrong?" Rich's dad muttered, angry that Rich had opened the door to the enemy.

Suddenly the Holy Spirit stopped him in his tracks. *You minister forgiveness to him until he finds repentance!* Immediately, Rich's father bowed his head and repented of any word or deed that had contributed to Rich's rebellion. He prayed, releasing forgiveness to his son, asking that forgiveness would cover Rich until he found repentance.

Three times that night Rich died. Three times CPR was initiated, and three times he revived. Six hours after the family had been told that Rich wouldn't survive the night, the doctor brought another report. "Whatever you're doing, keep doing it, because it's working."

Sunrise signified victory to the weary prayer warriors who had maintained their vigil all night. Although he was locked in a coma, Rich was still alive, and his vital signs were stable. Still, the doctors explained, he was paralyzed.

Rich's parents refused to believe that report. Instead, they claimed Jeremiah 30:17—a word the Lord gave Rich's best friend Tom Phelps—as God's will for Rich: *"'For I will restore you to health And I will heal you of your wounds,' declares the Lord..."(New American Standard).*

"We brought Scripture tapes to the hospital," Elaine explains, "and played them to Rich literally around the clock.

"A blood clot had formed on the right side of Rich's brain. The surgeon hesitated to operate on it because it was located in the part that controls speech. However, two weeks into the coma the blood clot was still enlarging and the surgery couldn't be postponed."

Once again the Sprenkels paced outside of surgery, praying. When the tedious surgery was over, the neurosurgeon stepped out to talk to Rich's family.

"Rich made it through the surgery," the doctor said, "but the damage was extensive. He won't be able to talk...in fact, he'll be a vegetable."

Rich's father shook the surgeon's hand. "My Lord is an awesome God," he explained. "Rich will be fine."

Later, he paced the corridor praying, "I thank You, Lord, for Rich's total and complete healing...spirit, soul and body."

Day after day passed with no change in Rich's condition. His father refused to go to work, choosing rather to stay near his son almost around the clock.

Twenty-eight days into the coma, the nurses noticed signs that Rich was about to regain consciousness. Family, friends and medical staff gathered around Rich's bed. The room was chillingly quiet when he opened his eyes and looked around. The boy destined to be "a vegetable" had a knowing look in his eye. And despite the medical predictions that he would never speak again, he opened his mouth.

"Thank you all for helping me," he said. "I love you. Could everybody leave now, please? I need to talk to my dad.

"Dad," Rich said, tears running down his cheeks, "I'm so sorry. Does God still love me? I want to tell Him I'm sorry for the way I've been living my life. Would you pray with me?"

Rich Sprenkel Sr. held his son and wept.

That afternoon Rich was transferred out of intensive care. Still heavily medicated, nurses and doctors were amazed once more. Rich could move his arms!

"Dad," Rich asked, trying desperately to move his legs, "am I going to be paralyzed?"

"No, son, and let me show you why," Mr. Sprenkel answered, opening the Bible. For days he taught his son Scripture, spoon-feeding him his covenant rights in Jesus. Rich progressed so rapidly another set of X-rays was taken. His family waited breathlessly for the report.

"His spinal cord isn't severed anymore!" The staff at Enloe Memorial knew Mr. Sprenkel was right about one thing. Their God was awesome.

Rich was transferred to a rehabilitation hospital where he worked to regain his strength. He'd lost 55 pounds during his hospitalization and had to relearn how to walk. But one tottering step after another, walk he did.

After two months of rehabilitation, Rich Sprenkel was discharged from the hospital. He still wore the "halo" that had been inserted to support his broken neck. The metal device was screwed into his forehead in two places and into the back of his head in two places.

"I went to see my doctor for a checkup," Rich says, "and when he saw the X-ray, he scheduled me for surgery at 8 o'clock the next morning. One of the broken vertebra had slipped and was almost on my spinal cord. It could actually *re-sever* my spinal cord.

"I was so upset I asked my dad why God had taken my healing away. He said God hadn't taken anything away, but that Satan wanted to steal my miracle. That evening Dad took me to a Bible study led by a Christian doctor. The people showed me what the Bible had to say about my healing, then they anointed me with oil and prayed that my vertebrae would be healed. I was baptized in the Holy Spirit and it felt like hot oil had been poured down my neck. That night I slept like a baby."

The following morning Rich went to the hospital alone. The surgeon met him prior to the surgery and asked if he was ready.

"No," Rich answered, "I don't need surgery, Doctor. I was anointed with oil and prayed for last night."

The stunned doctor laughed. "Well, I've seen you come this far, so I don't doubt that you're right. Let's take another X-ray."

Rich sat in the doctor's office for 20 minutes while the X-ray was developed. There on the wall was a lighted viewer which displayed the film of Rich's neck taken the day before. It didn't take a medical degree to see the broken vertebra which had slipped to a dangerous angle. When the doctor returned, he slipped the new X-ray beside the previous one. It was perfect.

"Rich made it through the surgery," the doctor said, "but the damage was extensive. He won't be able to talk...in fact, he'll be a vegetable."

The doctor studied each film and shook his head. "Let's cancel surgery and remove that halo," he said.

"Three months later," Rich recalls, "I was flipping through the television channels when I saw the New York City Marathon. I remember thinking, *Twenty-six and a half miles! Those people must be crazy!* Just then I felt the same hot oil like I'd felt the night I was baptized in the Holy Spirit. I heard the Lord say, *This is what you're going to do.* At that moment the desire to run a marathon was birthed in me."

Nine months after Rich's accident, the doctors said he could run. Rich tied on running shoes and did just that. He made it a half mile.

But Rich had learned something about the Lord and about His Word. Claiming Isaiah 40:31, *"They that wait upon the Lord shall renew their strength; they shall mount up with wings as eagles; they shall run, and not be weary; and they shall walk, and not faint,"* Rich continued to run.

One and a half years after watching the New York City Marathon on television, Rich entered the Chico Bidwell Classic Marathon. Among the spectators were Rich's friends, family and 12 nurses who'd cared for him in the hospital. Rich ran 26½ grueling miles. The time on the clock as he sprinted to finish was 2:59:53. Rich Sprenkel had just qualified for the Boston Marathon.

The press grabbed the story. Magazines, newspapers and television stations called. The Boston Marathon is one of the toughest races in the world. Few 20-year-olds qualify. None who'd been paralyzed just the year before. Rich agreed to the interviews on one condition: they tell the story of his miraculous healing.

"When I stepped off the plane in Boston," Rich recalls, "I felt the anointing again and I began to weep. Instead of lying paralyzed in a hospital somewhere, I was in Boston competing in one of the most prestigious races in the world."

Race day dawned clear and bright. One and a half million spectators lined the streets or watched by television. Eight thousand runners gathered at the starting line. Rich drank in the sights and sounds, his heart pounding from heady excitement.

Rich prayed when the race started, "Lord, I commit

my running to You. Lift me up on wings as eagles that I would not faint..."

Rich Sprenkel ran shoulder to shoulder with professional runners and Olympic athletes, finishing the race in the top 20 percent.

Today, Rich competes in marathons, triathlons and long-distance bicycle races. Wherever he goes, he tells of God's miraculous power. When he isn't racing, Rich uses watercolors to paint the glorious world around him.

Whether it's a marathon, or participating in an art show, Rich Sprenkel knows that each step of his feet and each stroke of the brush is testimony of his own race for a miracle.

Update: Rich continues to enjoy a completely restored body. He is still experiencing victory in all the areas of his life as reflected in this account.

Rich has been a Partner with Kenneth Copeland Ministries for 3 years! And his parents have been Partners for 19 years!

When Time Moved Ahead in Green Valley

by Melanie Hemry

Floye Vastine stood at the door of her home in Kentucky on August 6, 1991, and looked out across 93 acres of family land. She'd always thought of this as her own "green valley." Located in the heart of the Appalachian hill country, it nestled snugly between the Cumberland and the Kentucky Rivers.

An angel could put a foot in each river and straddle this valley, she thought whimsically.

Floye liked to think about angels. Perhaps because she was widowed and the knowledge of their presence especially comforted her. Or, perhaps because she knew she needed their help to watch after her two grandsons, Richard and Michael.

At 10 and 11 years old, they were a handful. No doubt about that! But she'd managed to keep up with them ever since they began living with her nine years ago. And, by the grace of God, she intended to keep right on seeing to it they were raised and raised right—in the nurture and admonition of the Lord.

Smiling, Floye stood for a moment and listened to the deep grumble of the tractor as it echoed toward the house from the direction of the barn. Then she turned and went inside to begin her chores—peacefully assured her angels were standing guard that day and totally unaware of just how desperately she was going to need them.

As Floye's son-in-law, Stevie Gibson, steered the tractor through the barn door, he glanced up at the low-hanging metal rails that stretched across the barn ceiling. Then he took a look behind him.

Sure enough, there was 11-year-old Michael perched happily on the back of the tractor. No surprise. Ever since Stevie had begun helping Floye around the farm, Michael had loved to catch an impromptu ride now and then.

"Duck, Mike! Those rails are low!" Stevie yelled. Obediently, Michael grabbed the tractor's roll bar for support and ducked his head as they passed under a 2-by-6 rail.

Later, as Stevie fired up the tractor and headed out of the barn, he once again glanced back to check for Michael. But Mike hadn't hitched his usual ride this time. He was simply standing there watching. Assured that Michael was safely behind him, Stevie guided the tractor out of the cool, shadowy barn into the bright August sun.

As he did, the peaceful air of "green valley" was shattered by Michael's screams.

It happened in a split second.

Michael making a quick last-minute jump onto the back of the tractor...Michael ducking to miss the rail too late...Michael being jerked from his feet and forced headfirst through the 2½-inch space between the rail and the roll bar.

"Michael!" Stevie cried in horror. But it was too late.

The scene that met Floye was like a gruesome nightmare that wouldn't end. The left side of Michael's face was totally flattened. The bridge of his nose was shoved a half inch into his skull. His left eye had been displaced. His nostrils were ripped away and every time his heart beat, blood spurted from his nose.

"The instant I saw Michael," she recalls, "fear gripped me. But I said, 'Devil, you are a liar! God has not given me a spirit of fear, but of love and a sound mind!' I bound the spirit of fear and I bound the flow of blood. I loosed the Holy Spirit to minister healing and I loosed the angels to minister to Michael."

With no hospitals nearby and no ambulance service available, Floye was forced to put Michael in the car and drive him to the nearest doctor's office in Williamsburg, Kentucky. When she got there, it was closed.

"I'm not going to make it, am I?" Michael gasped when they pulled away from the clinic.

"Yes, you *will* make it, Michael," Floye answered firmly. "According to Luke 10:19, I have power over the devil and nothing can harm me. Furthermore, according to Isaiah 54, the fruit of my womb is blessed. My children are blessed! My grandchildren are blessed!"

Floye's car sped across the 11 miles to Jellico Tennessee Community Hospital. There, doctors treated Michael for shock.

Showing Floye his X-rays, they detailed Michael's injuries. The displacement of bones was dramatic. The space between the bridge of his nose and his right eye measured 12 centimeters. The same space to his left eye measured 21 centimeters. His nose was broken. The sinuses were torn away. Both cheekbones were fractured. Michael's palate had been shattered like a windshield hit by a bullet. His jaw and teeth had been realigned.

"We can't help him here," the doctor explained. "He needs specialists and major plastic and reconstructive surgery. We're sending Michael to Oak Ridge, Tennessee." Another 54 miles.

"This is one lucky young man," the specialist told Floye when they reached Oak Ridge.

"No, doctor, he's blessed," Floye responded.

"Call it what you like," the doctor replied, "but I can tell you, his neck should have been broken instantly. I've never seen an injury like this where the neck *wasn't* broken."

Although the Oak Ridge doctor confirmed that Michael needed massive surgery to reconstruct his face, there was a problem. The hospital was full.

"There was nothing else for us to do," says Floye, "so after they treated Michael, we had to go home for the night. We were to have him back for surgery at 8 o'clock the next morning. It was 1 o'clock in the morning when we got home. I never even went to bed. I stayed up and rejected every evil report spoken over Michael and paced the house praying in the Spirit."

Early the next morning, the phone rang. The hospital was still full. Surgery had to be postponed two days. The doctor said waiting would help the swelling diminish and make the surgery more successful. The devil, however, had other plans.

"The next day the outside temperature rose to 103 degrees," Floye recalls. "My house isn't air conditioned so I positioned a fan beside a pan of ice, hoping the cool air blowing on Michael would cool him down. Even so, the heat caused his face to swell so much that the skin stretched and seeped. His lips swelled inside out and cracked. His eyes swelled closed. He couldn't breathe through his nose at all.

"My pastor, Rev. G.S. Bowling, had been praying with the men in our church for a miracle. Family and friends flocked to the house to pray. That afternoon I heard someone say 'Michael's getting worse by the minute. He's not going to make it.'

"When I heard that, I stormed into that room and climbed onto Michael's bed. 'Doubt and unbelief leave this room!' I said. 'According to the Word of God, Michael will live and not die! God will raise him up for His glory!'"

Michael's father arrived at 4 o'clock the next morning. He took one look at his son and loaded him into the car. "He's going back to the hospital now!" he said. "We're not waiting any longer."

When the doctors at Oak Ridge saw Michael's condition, they took him immediately into surgery. For 5½ hours, they rebuilt his palate and wired his teeth, jaws and cheekbones back together. After surgery, Michael was sent to the intensive care unit. The surgeon said his recovery would require six weeks to three months in the hospital along with plastic surgery.

When Floye stepped into the ICU cubicle, she gasped at the sight of her grandson. The left side of his face was still marred and misshapen. His color was as white as the stark sheet that draped him. A respirator forced air into his lungs.

Floye didn't know much about medicine. But she knew her rights—and this wasn't right! This wasn't her heritage as a believer. She had been a Christian for 40 years. She'd been a Partner with Kenneth and Gloria Copeland for 17 years. She believed in miracles. Now she needed one.

"I fell to my knees at the foot of Michael's bed right there in ICU," Floye explains. "I said, 'Lord, this isn't what Your Word says. Four hundred and thirty years before Christ, Isaiah looked down and saw a man Whose visage was so marred, He no longer resembled a man. And in Isaiah 53:5, he wrote, with His stripes we are healed.

"'After Jesus was raised from the dead, Peter looked back at the cross and wrote, by Whose stripes ye *were* healed. Lord, either Your Word is true or the last 40 years of my life have been a lie. I believe Your Word!'"

Floye began praying in the Spirit and soon a Presence filled the room. Suddenly, she remembered the Syrophenician woman who petitioned Jesus for a miracle for her daughter (Mark 7:25-30). Jesus had initially told that woman, *"Let the children first be filled: for it is not meet to take the children's bread, and cast it unto the dogs."*

But the woman had persisted. *"Yes, Lord: yet the dogs under the table eat of the children's crumbs."* That answer of faith got her the miracle she wanted.

> "The instant I saw Michael, fear gripped me. But I said, 'Devil, you are a liar!'"

"I started thinking," Floye says, "even though it wasn't yet time for the gentiles, because of that woman's faith, *God moved time ahead for her child!* So I prayed and asked God to hear my faith and move time ahead for Michael."

One hour later, family members gathered around Michael's bed. What they saw left them speechless. His face was no longer flat and misshapen. Hour by hour his features appeared to shift. The next morning he was moved out of intensive care.

Michael began to recover so rapidly that instead of being discharged in three months—he was discharged in three more *days.*

"When Michael went back for his two-week checkup," Floye remembers, "the doctor used tweezers to gently peel the skin off his face. Underneath was perfect, pink skin. No scars. The doctor was absolutely astounded. Michael didn't need any plastic surgery."

Students at Michael's school began classes on August 14—just eight days after his accident. One day later, on August 15, he joined them. Basketball season began as usual. And in October, Michael—named the school's most valuable basketball player the year before—was back on the team.

"I was praying not long after that," says Floye, "when I heard something in my spirit. I didn't whisper a word of it to anyone. I said, 'Lord, if I heard You right, confirm it through one of Your prophets.' The next Sunday night, a minister called Michael forward and anointed him with oil. He repeated the same words I'd heard in prayer. He said, 'Michael, you're called of God to preach the gospel to your generation.'"

Months later at a revival, Charles Capps called Michael forward and said, "He Who began a good work in you will perform it until the day of Jesus Christ."

And He has. Today, Michael is a healthy, happy 12-year-old. Many say he looks 15. Maybe that's because, for a while, God moved time ahead for Michael at the insistence of one faithful grandmother from green valley.

Update: The call of God on Michael's life continues to be evident. As a totally healed young man, Michael recently ministered with his church youth group during a week of camp. Under the anointing, he laid hands on others and saw the power of God move on them. Four pastors have prophesied over him as well, that he will preach the gospel to his generation.

Floye has been a Partner with Kenneth Copeland Ministries for 18 years!

CHAPTER 4

Testimonies of Prosperity

*"He who pursues righteousness and love
finds life, prosperity and honor."*

Proverbs 21:21, New International Version

You Never Know Where a Dream Might Lead

by Melanie Hemry

*O*UT OF BUSINESS. Ed Goss stood on the steps of the Truck Driving Academy and stared in shock at the sign posted.

"No!!" He tried the door. Locked. The coffee he'd guzzled to keep him awake during his hours of studying stirred bitterly in his stomach as thoughts of the past few months tumbled through his mind. *Weeks of studying all night. Weary days on the job. Long hours preparing for tests. The tuition he'd paid...money he and his wife Charla desperately needed just to survive. All of it had been wasted!*

Ed turned away from the door. There was nothing to do but go home. Ed had known it wouldn't be easy for a black man to climb out of the quicksand of poverty in Oklahoma in 1973. He knew he'd have to have a dream to do it. And he did. It wasn't a big dream by most standards—he just wanted to drive a truck.

But now, so close to his dream, Ed was out of time. He was out of tuition. He was out of business.

"Everything began to unravel," Ed remembers. "I was a Christian, but I wasn't walking with the Lord."

For Charla, however, spiritually things were just beginning to come together. The year before she had found a Bible in the closet, read it and was born again. She had quickly developed an unquenchable appetite for the Word. So, when she stumbled onto the biblical truth of tithing, she and Ed immediately began giving the local church $20 of their meager $200-a-week income.

They expected God to bless them for it and He did. Within months, Ed was accepted into a truck driver training program offered by the Lee Way Freight Company. By May of 1974, he had graduated from the program and his dream had become reality.

"We were in tall cotton," Ed recalls. "When I began driving for Lee Way my salary doubled. In August, Charla resigned from her job to stay at home full time with our son."

Only three months later however, disappointment struck again. Lee Way announced a layoff. Ed was out of work.

Immediately he began searching for a job with another trucking company. But no one would hire him. They simply couldn't insure a driver with less than two years of experience. Ed had only driven for six months. "Sorry," he was told again and again, "that's just the way it is."

In desperation, they applied for unemployment. Their combined unemployment checks totaled $150 each week. They tithed the first $15.

Even though things looked hopeless, the Gosses knew there was somewhere they could turn for help. The Word of God. For the past few months Charla had been listening to Kenneth Copeland's radio broadcast and spending hours a day in prayer and Bible study.

During one of her prayer times the Lord had spoken to her heart. *I'm going to teach you to live by faith,* He said, *one day at a time.* Clearly the time had arrived for that teaching to begin.

Searching the Scriptures, Ed and Charla discovered Matthew 18:19, *"...if two of you agree on earth about anything that they may ask, it shall be done for them by My Father who is in heaven" (New American Standard).*

If any two agree.... The Word said they could have what they agreed for in prayer. It didn't say, *you can have it, unless you're black.* It didn't say, *you can have it, unless you're poor.* Suddenly Ed and Charla Goss understood they'd never be a minority again. If the two of them would stand in agreement with God and His Word, they would *always* be the majority.

They agreed in prayer that God would meet all their needs. They agreed that He would give them favor with their creditors.

Nothing seemed to change. Weeks dragged into months. Eventually, even the flow of cash from the unemployment checks dried up.

"I always considered myself to be the spiritual one," Charla admits. "But Ed was out of work for a year and a half. When we were cashing our last check— I panicked. I said, 'Neither of us has a job! This is our *last check!* What are we doing to do?'"

Ed's easy smile faded. "If you had your faith in those checks all this time," he said, "you missed it a long time ago. The Lord will take care of us."

Sure enough, He did. A week later the phone rang at 5 a.m. Lee Way was rehiring its drivers. Ed had his job back!

During the following year, the Gosses settled happily into their newly found prosperity. They bought a house. Their 7-year-old started school, and Charla became pregnant with their second child. It was wonderful...but already Ed was beginning to dream again.

"He came home one day and said he was thinking about quitting his job," Charla says. "He wanted to buy a truck and start his own business."

Charla listened in horror. She was pregnant! They

had a house payment! He wanted to leave a $35,000-a-year job! She opened her mouth to tell Ed just what she thought about his idea, but the voice of the Holy Spirit stopped her. *Don't discourage him...you never know where a dream might lead.* Charla choked back her negative words.

"When I prayed about it," Charla recalls, "the Lord showed me that it wasn't my responsibility to be the provider—that was Ed's job. Mine was to get into agreement with him."

The next two years passed peacefully as Ed continued to work for Lee Way and nurture his dream. Then, one blustery day in November 1980, he left Oklahoma City on a truck run to California. When he arrived there, he called Charla. "This is my last trip," he told her. "I'm quitting Lee Way and buying a truck."

Charla gripped the phone. Their 2-year-old son, Chris, tugged on her leg while the devil tugged on her mind. *No savings. No job. No income. Don't let him....*

The quiet voice of the Holy Spirit spoke again. *Don't discourage him... you never know....*

"I'm with you," Charla said. "Let's pray."

"I always considered myself to be the spiritual one," Charla admits. "But Ed was out of work for a year and a half. When we were cashing our last check—I panicked. I said, 'Neither of us has a job! This is our *last check!* What are we going to do?'"

The following week, Ed walked into the Kenworth dealership and offered to buy a $70,000 rig. "Fine," the dealer said, "just give us $1,000 earnest money, and we'll start the credit report." Ed wrote the check.

"We needed $16,000 down," Ed explains, "and another $4,000 for fuel and tarps. The dealer was going to call my bank the next day to verify that I had $16,000 in my account. The problem was, I didn't. I knew how I could get the money, but the arrangements would take some time. Charla and I prayed the prayer of agreement and asked the Lord to supply what we needed."

Go talk to your banker, the Lord said. *I'll give you favor.*

Hours later, Ed was at the bank, explaining the situation.

"I'll tell you what I'll do," the banker said. "I'll put $16,000 of my own money in your account until yours comes."

A banker is putting his own money in my account! Thank God—that's favor!

As soon as they bought the truck, the Gosses drove it to church and dedicated it to God. Ed formed a partnership with another Christian businessman creating one of the first black-owned freight companies in Oklahoma.

The Lord continued to give them favor. With Ed as president, the company doubled its income every year. Other trucks were added, rail freight was added, the business expanded to Detroit and other areas. But to Ed, that first Kenworth truck would always represent God's faithfulness.

"After 200,000 miles I had the wheels pulled to check the brakes," Ed recalls. "They weren't even worn. Nothing on that truck ever wore out."

During those years, Ed and Charla continued to tithe and give, but they didn't stop there. They took another giant step of faith as well. For five years they tithed—not on their present income but on the expanded income they *desired* to receive!

Then, in May of 1990, the Lord directed Ed to resign from the company he started and step out once again on faith and faith alone.

"There's a business for sale in Detroit," Ed told Charla, "Art Brockman, Inc. They're a specialized heavy-haul company. I think we're going to buy it."

"How much?" Charla asked.

"They're asking $3.6 million," Ed explained.

Three million dollars. Charla remembered when it took all their faith to believe for $70,000. She looked around their home, a beautiful rock house nestled on several wooded acres with a swimming pool. There had been a time when they couldn't have imagined living in such a place. They had exercised their spiritual muscles a lot since then, and they knew their Father even better.

Don't discourage him, the familiar words began, *you never know where a dream might lead.*

"I'm with you," Charla said. "Let's pray."

"At the time, I had bills on my desk totaling $3,000," Ed recalls. "The last check from my previous job was for $350. I looked at the check and looked at my bills, then I tithed the whole amount. One thing I had learned from Brother Copeland was that man could control my salary, but only God controlled my income."

Ed made an offer on the business, hoping to buy it within four months. He figured he could hold out that long without a salary.

$600,000. That was the amount they needed for the down payment. Of course, they didn't have it...but that was nothing new. Ed and Charla knew from experience exactly what to do about that. They would simply ask their heavenly Father for what they needed, set their faith and receive!

They didn't expect it to be easy. Nothing worthwhile ever was. Yet even so, they never suspected how viciously the devil would fight to keep them out of the multimillion-dollar league. It never occurred to them the battle would last for almost a year.

Month after grueling month, Ed spent his weekdays in Detroit working out one problem...just to run into another. At times it seemed he was trapped in an endless maze filled with bankers, lawyers, board meetings, frustrations and disappointments. What's more, with Charla at home in Oklahoma with their sons, Ed was running that maze alone.

"After months of intense spiritual battle," Charla says, "I knew Ed needed more reinforcement than I could give him on the telephone. A friend of ours gave him the complete set of tapes from KCM's 1991 West Coast Believers' Convention. Ed listened to them constantly."

Finally, the breakthrough came. Every obstacle bowed to Jesus' Name and in February 1991, Ed and Charla Goss became the owners of the Brockman company. When the sale was complete, they drove to an automatic teller machine to check the balance of their account. It showed $2.47.

Yet, during all those months of negotiations, they paid their tithe, gave to their church building program, maintained their home in Oklahoma, an apartment in Detroit, traveled between the two places regularly and hired a staff of lawyers. They did it without a salary—but never without an income.

Today, Ed runs a multimillion-dollar company. Charla, now an ordained minister, spreads the word of faith and supports Ed in prayer.

Recently, Ed came home with a gleam in his eye.

"Remember when the Lord told me to expand into air freight?" he asked. Charla remembered. "Well," Ed explained, "I've found an airline for sale."

Charla gazed into the brilliant blue sky, vast with possibilities. "I'm with you," she said, reaching for Ed's hand. "Let's pray."

After all, you never know where a dream might lead.

Update: In 1991, when Ed and Charla bought Art Brockman, Inc., they dreamed of owning a trucking company, and expanding into air freight. Since then, the Gosses have traveled to Haiti and Jamaica to help establish medical and evangelism teams.

Today, their dream has changed from running a business in the United States, to traveling with mission teams to third world countries.

In July of 1995, Art Brockman, Inc. was sold, and Ed and Charla returned to Oklahoma City. Life has changed drastically for Ed Goss, who started his walk of faith by driving trucks across country. Now his ambitions lead him to win souls in Africa, the Caribbean and the West Indies.

Ed and Charla have been Partners with Kenneth Copeland Ministries for 10 years!

An Investment of the Heart

by Melanie Hemry

Dog collars, and more dog collars. Some days Bill Pantin didn't think he could stand the sight of one more dog collar. On days like today he felt as though life had collared *him!*

For three years he'd spent every working day in this factory making dog collars. He had worked his way up all the way to rivet-man. Three long years...and his greatest achievement was putting the right number of rivets in a dog collar!

Big deal, Bill shook his head and stamped another rivet. Something was stirring inside of him. Something in him wanted *out.* He wanted more out of life. He knew he wasn't particularly bright. He'd figured that out for himself back in high school and during his first venture into college.

Those experiences proved what his dad had told him all along, "You'll never do anything in life." Still, he *had* worked his way up to rivet-man.

Thud. Another rivet slammed into place. And another. Rhythmically, hypnotically, Bill moved the collars through. He thought about the family who had recently befriended him. They knew about struggling through life too, yet they had given Bill something he'd never known—affirmation. He especially received love from the mother, a born-again woman who knew what wonders Jesus could do with a life like his. She talked to him about college. *You can do it!* Her words tantalized him. *Make something of your life!* Could he?

On a sunny day in late 1979, as he stamped out his final few rivets, Bill dared to answer that question. Walking away from the assembly line, he looked his foreman in the eye and said two words that would change the entire course of his life. "I quit."

"I grew up behind an eight ball," Bill says. "I was raised in a middle-class family in a not-so-nice part of Long Island. I had a real attitude. I didn't know much, but I did know I didn't want to rivet dog collars for the rest of my life."

With the tedium of his job behind him, Bill wasted no time. He immediately arranged for a student loan and enrolled in a state university. Driven by the fear of failure, he pushed himself by taking 21 hours per semester.

Although Bill had accepted his born-again friend's advice to go to college...he hadn't accepted her Jesus. So at school, he found himself very much alone.

"I didn't know the Lord," Bill explains. "I'd been raised Catholic, but I had never returned to church after my confirmation at age 12. During those first months at college, a Christian lived across the hall from me. I read his tracts and attended a church service once or twice. It just didn't take."

But a seed was planted. By December 1980, Bill was physically and emotionally exhausted. Not knowing where to turn, he prayed.

"I said, 'Lord, I need some help.' Suddenly, total love washed over me. I lost the sense of where I was. I didn't know who I was. The love so consumed me that I thought I'd die."

The experience only lasted five minutes, but the refreshing lasted much longer. Back at school, he pursued his goal—and he achieved it. In only 2¹/₂ years, Bill graduated—with honors.

Still, he wasn't content. Plowing ahead, Bill earned his graduate degree in international affairs, international economics and Latin American studies. The world of rivets and dog collars faded like a bad dream. Bill was finally climbing the ladder of success. And meeting Christina in 1985 was another step up.

They were an unlikely pair from the start. Born in Malaysia, Christina was one of five children from a wealthy Chinese family. Unlike Bill's no-frills upbringing, Christina's was awash in luxury. She was beautiful, smart—and accustomed to getting her way. She intimidated every man she met. But Bill was a New Yorker. Nothing intimidated him. They married in 1987.

Together, their success continued. Christina earned her bachelor's degree in journalism and her graduate degree in international affairs. The British news agency Reuters hired her, and she later became its senior stock market reporter. Bill worked for a financial services company. They had it all...careers, money and a plush apartment in a fancy Manhattan high-rise.

They made it on their own. They didn't know God and they didn't need Him. Until 1989 when their sweet success was soured by a bad economy.

The downturn literally brought Bill to his knees. "There was a layoff," Bill explains, "and I lost my job. Every day when Christina left for work, I stayed home combing the want ads. Depression hit hard. All my insecurities flared."

You can't even support your wife, sneered a silent voice inside Bill's mind. *Go back to making dog collars.*

A few weeks later, Bill was flipping through the television channels when his attention was captured by a man in a sweater talking intently to the television audience. Just as he started to change channels, Bill heard something that stopped him. Something that changed his life. The man on the television screen was Kenneth Copeland. The words he spoke were these: "You can have what you say."

"I watched that program," Bill says, "and I was intrigued. I'd never heard anything like it. A couple of weeks later I heard Kenneth say each person needed to accept Jesus as Lord and receive the Baptism in the Holy Spirit." In response, Bill Pantin knelt beside the bed and gave his heart to Jesus. It would prove to be the wisest investment he ever made.

A few days later, Bill prayed again, asking the Lord to direct his life. To his surprise, God answered in an audible voice.

"I plant a seed so that it will grow to feed My children," He said.

Three long years... and his greatest achievement was putting the right number of rivets in a dog collar!

Bill had never read the Bible. He'd never heard the parable of planting and reaping. He whispered the words over and over. God wanted him to plant seeds and feed children? Was he being called into...agriculture? Confused, he shook his head. He could only hope that God would explain Himself more thoroughly as time went along.

"Then one day," Bill explains, "I opened the *New York Times* to read the want ads. The Holy Spirit spoke to me and said, *There is a job inside just for you.*"

Searching the newsprint, Bill gasped at what he found. Mitsubishi Bank, Ltd. wanted someone with his qualifications. *The fourth largest bank in the world!* "I prayed the prayer of faith," Bill remembers, "and called for an interview. The interview went well, but I was told that Japanese banks don't act quickly. It would be weeks before I heard.

"At 10 o'clock that morning I prayed according to Mark 11:24 that I would hear a good report that very day."

By 5 o'clock, the devil was working overtime to discourage Bill. *People have gone home now. You blew it. This faith stuff doesn't work.* But as usual, the devil was just bluffing. At 6 o'clock the telephone rang. Bill Pantin had landed the job.

Even so, Christina was skeptical about the changes in Bill. "I couldn't believe that he was watching Kenneth Copeland's broadcast. On Sundays he'd sit there glued to the television while I read the newspaper. Then I began to see results. After a few months I couldn't argue anymore. I prayed, making Jesus Lord of my life, and received the Baptism in the Holy Spirit."

Inspired by the Copelands' teachings, Bill and Christina began to study the Bible six to seven hours a day. They'd get up early to pray and read the Bible. On the subway they'd listen to tapes. During the day, they recorded the Copelands' program to watch each evening. After supper they prayed and went back to reading the Bible. In bed at night, they read books on faith.

Eagerly, they began to apply what they were learning to every area of their lives. At home and on the job, they began to step out in faith.

"I was told, for example, that Mitsubishi wouldn't promote an employee to assistant vice president until he'd worked there for five or six years," Bill explains. "But Christina and I prayed in agreement that I would receive the promotion in one year."

When Bill received his yearly review he was told he did not have the promotion he desired. Boldly, he wrote one word across the bottom of the review document: Unacceptable. At home, he and Christina praised God for the promotion, continuing to stand in faith. Three days later he became assistant vice president at Mitsubishi Bank Ltd.

Faith even invaded Bill's daily commute to the office. He recalls one day in particular. He was riding the subway to work—listening to tapes as usual—when a burly construction worker boarded the subway, sat down and began to doze.

Unexpectedly, the Lord spoke to Bill. *Tell him that he has delighted in Me, now I'll give him the desires of his heart. Tell him you know he has problems now, but it will all work out.*

"But God, you don't understand. You don't tell construction workers things like this on a New York subway."

Tell him.

"I'm going to change subways."

Tell him. Bill looked up. The woman who had occupied the seat next to the construction worker had left the subway. Reluctantly, Bill moved to her vacant seat and began, "Excuse me," he said, "but God told me to tell you...." Finishing the words, Bill looked into the big man's face.

The man grabbed Bill's hands and said, "Thank you, Brother. My wife has a brain aneurysm. I have four kids I'm trying to take care of and I'm hardly getting any sleep."

When Bill changed to his next subway, he wept. For the first time in his life he knew for certain that he'd been created for something more important than making dog collars.

And he understood that the Word and the anointing is the seed that, when planted, will grow and feed God's children.

As that anointing kept on growing, the Pantins' lives changed dramatically. But one thing stayed the same. God continued to use their partnership with Kenneth Copeland Ministries to bring God's blessing and direction to their lives.

"For a long time we didn't have a church," Christina explains. "We'd moved out of Manhattan into a very nice Jewish neighborhood. There weren't any faith churches around. Bill had heard about a church in Long Island where Jerry Savelle spoke. It was called Faith of God's Word Ministry and was pastored by Dan and Janet Cotrone. We prayed for guidance regarding the church and decided to contact them as soon as we returned from KCM's Southwest Believers' Convention in Fort Worth.

As it turned out, they didn't have to wait that long.

During the convention, Bill and Christina found themselves seated next to a young couple who were also from New York. Their name? COTRONE. The son and daughter-in-law of Dan and Janet Cotrone, the couple attended Faith of God's Word Ministry. Thanking God for His guidance, Bill and Christina found their church home.

Today, Bill and Christina Pantin are enjoying a supernatural success that's sweeter than they've ever known. And as the economy continues to pitch and roll, they simply keep on prospering. The reason, says Bill, is simple.

"One of the first things we learned was to tithe and give. And God has proven Himself faithful. When the writers union was without an agreement with management, all the writers at Christina's company went without raises or promotions for over a year.

"All, that is, except Christina. During that time she

received two promotions and one merit raise. When the new contract was negotiated she received a 13$^1/_2$ percent increase—retroactive."

During the past three years Bill's income has increased an average of 25 percent per year. Today, he manages a $1.1 billion loan portfolio for Latin America. He earns a six-figure salary and every penny of it is a return on the investment of faith he began to make that unforgettable day in 1989 when he knelt beside his bed and prayed.

Thinking back to his dog collar days, Bill smiles at how far he's come. And the advice that dear Christian lady gave him 13 years ago still echoes in his ears. *Make something of your life.* "Yeah," he says. "Give it to Jesus. You'll be amazed what He can do."

Update: The account in this article was just the beginning of the mighty works God has done in Bill and Christina's lives. Since then, they have moved to Fort Worth, Texas, where Bill has attended and graduated from Jerry Savelle's Bible Institute and School of World Evangelism.

Through miraculous circumstances, Christina transferred from Reuters in New York to be the bureau chief of their Dallas office covering North Texas, Oklahoma, New Mexico and Arkansas. And in the fall of 1995, they moved to Malaysia where Bill, as an ordained minister, preaches the gospel to the poor and needy, and to the decision makers and financial leaders of Southeast Asian nations. Christina is deputy bureau chief of Reuters in Malaysia—another blessing that God arranged.

What Bill learned in business is that to more than double your money in investments is beyond normal expectations. But he has learned firsthand, that when God makes an investment, He always expects and reaps a hundredfold return.

Bill and Christina have been Partners with Kenneth Copeland Ministries for 7 years!

Award-Winning Faith

by Melanie Hemry

Teresa Gallman herded her class of first grade students onto a bus for the 65-mile drive to Jacksonville, Florida. To some people, it might have seemed too far to go just to see a play at the Children's Theatre, but not to Teresa. She was determined to give her students the chance to stretch beyond the artistic bounds of Woodbine, Georgia.

Although it was a wonderful community, Woodbine had distinctly limited cultural opportunities. Nestled on the bank of the Satilla River, Woodbine sported one stoplight, a country store and a grocery. The closest movie theater was 20 miles away, and at Woodbine Elementary, coloring was the students' only exposure to art.

Teresa looked out the window at the long-needle pines and smiled ruefully. Here she was trying to solve problems for her students, yet she didn't even have answers for her own life. When she considered the shattering effects of her recent divorce, the responsibility of raising two teenagers alone, and her staggering financial problems, Teresa felt she'd made disappointingly low grades in the course called life.

After the play, Teresa took her students to a nearby park for lunch. Unwrapping the sandwich she'd brought from home, she mused aloud, "It's a shame the children have to travel so far just to be exposed to the arts. There must be a way to bring art to Woodbine."

"Sure," another teacher said, laughing, "and maybe you'll win a million dollars in the lottery."

"I don't need a million," Teresa countered with a grin, "$25,000 will be plenty."

The following morning Teresa awoke at 5:30. Fixing breakfast, she gazed out the kitchen window at the peaceful, wooded acres that surrounded her home. By 6 a.m. she was settled in front of the television.

Wrapped warmly in her robe and slippers, Teresa Gallman wasn't a teacher at this hour—she was a student. And, with the help of her newfound television teachers, Kenneth and Gloria Copeland, she was studying faith as diligently as her students studied their ABCs.

"I was desperate," Teresa says. "My children and my students were looking to me for answers that I didn't have. I knew God had those answers, but I hadn't learned to tap into them. Until I started listening to the Copelands, I didn't really grasp the promises that I was heir to in Jesus, and I had never understood the power of speaking faith-filled words.

"I quickly developed a habit of watching their broadcast every morning, and keeping praise and teaching tapes in my truck. Yet, even when I began believing and confessing that all my needs are met through Christ Jesus, things didn't change overnight. In fact, for a while my circumstances looked worse."

Looking back now, however, Teresa can see that even during those discouraging days, God's plan for her was already underway.

In September 1989, the principal of Woodbine Elementary called the teachers together to discuss the upcoming contest for the Christa McAuliffe Educator's Award. Every teacher in the nation was eligible to participate in the contest. The winners— two per state—would each receive $15,000 to use for a special project in his or her school system. To enter, each teacher had to write a proposal outlining a major problem in the school system and a plan to meet the need.

"Who knows," the principal said handing out the forms, "maybe one of you will win."

Sure, Teresa thought.

That evening she tossed the papers on the kitchen table and started her chores. Ideas began to take shape in her mind while she fed the horses. *Write it down,* the Holy Spirit urged.

That night Teresa began writing her proposal. She outlined the problems that Woodbine Elementary faced in a rural, economically depressed area of the county. She described the special problems of a regional school that drew students from miles away. She explained how students had to be transported for miles to gain any exposure to the arts. Finally, she designed an artist-in-residency program that would bring artists with differing mediums to Woodbine for a week each month. The artists would work with the students, teachers, and when possible, provide concerts or exhibitions for the community.

> God said that all her needs were met through Christ Jesus. That was the only reality that Teresa Gallman could afford.

"I turned in my proposal without another thought," Teresa recalls. "I knew there would be hundreds of entries, and more importantly, I knew that the award usually went to science projects—not art."

A few months later, Teresa was surprised to receive a phone call during class. She was even more surprised to hear a staff member of the

Georgia Superintendent of Education's office tell her she'd been chosen as one of the winners of the Christa McAuliffe Award.

"I was so excited, I was speechless," Teresa remembers. "Then it dawned on me that now I had to *do* everything I'd proposed. I was asked to open a new bank account in my name to handle the $15,000 winner's fee. The awards were set up so the money could be used only for the winning projects, and only the winners could spend the funds. No school board or principal or committee could divert the money.

"Ironically, I now had two bank accounts in my name, yet my personal finances hadn't changed. One balance was high, the other almost nonexistent. I could spend $15,000 on the school, but I couldn't buy my daughter a new pair of shoes."

News of Teresa's award spread through Woodbine like an oil-spill. Everywhere Teresa went people congratulated her. "What's next, Teresa," they called, "are you gonna win the million-dollar lottery?"

"Naw," Teresa replied, "I don't need a million dollars. Twenty-five thousand should do."

Rather than relieving the pressure in her life, Teresa's newfound success only seemed to add more. No longer did she just have to stretch every penny. Now she had to stretch every minute as well.

In addition to teaching first grade, raising two teenagers, taking care of her horses and property, Teresa began implementing her project. Soon artists began appearing at Woodbine Elementary. They came in all sizes and shapes: sketch artists, musicians, photographers, painters, potters, storytellers and puppeteers, all weaving their beauty through Woodbine.

Teresa sat up late one night paying bills. From one

account she paid for the artists' room and board, supplies and salaries. From the other she paid for her own mortgage, utilities, gas, clothes and food. She looked at the bills piled on her desk and sighed. How could she stretch a teacher's salary in so many directions?

"What are we gonna do, Mom?" her son asked, leaning over her shoulder.

"I don't know..." she began, then corrected herself. "We're going to do fine, Son, because our God supplies all of our needs through Christ Jesus," Teresa replied.

"Oh, Mom, get real. How can you say your needs are met when we don't have anything?"

Get real! That's what the devil told her every time she looked at her finances. For years Teresa believed that circumstances were real. But no more. She couldn't afford to believe that. Her circumstances were screaming that she wasn't going to make it. Circumstances looked like she and the kids were going to lose everything she'd worked so hard to get: the house, the land...everything.

But *God* said that all her needs were met through Christ Jesus. That was the only reality that Teresa Gallman could afford.

"By January of 1990—halfway through our artist-in-residency program—my personal finances were spinning out of control," Teresa admits. "I knew I needed the prayer of agreement and I needed it fast. One morning I caught my friend, Bridget, before school and asked her to pray with me.

"She began praying in tongues, then she said that the Holy Spirit showed her that He was going to move on me and my situation in a marvelous way. Although I didn't know how it would happen, that prayer helped me continue to stand."

For 10 months Teresa kept on confessing her faith in God's provision and praying over her bills. Then, in October 1990, Teresa was called out of class for another telephone call. This time, she heard the superintendent's voice on the line.

"Teresa," he said, "I'm pleased to inform you that you've been selected as a winner of the First Annual Georgia Educators' Award!"

Teresa sighed. *I wonder what I'll have to do now.*

"Just exactly what does that mean?" she asked.

"It means you've won $25,000."

"Praise the Lord!" Teresa exclaimed. "How am I supposed to use this money?"

"You don't understand what I'm saying," the superintendent said. "The money is from the Milkin Family Foundation in Los Angeles. It's purpose is to honor teachers. The money is *yours*. For your personal use."

$25,000. Someone is giving me $25,000! In the space of a heartbeat, Teresa could see it all. The bills paid...fences mended...money set aside for college. All her needs met by God's riches because she claimed her inheritance—the inheritance of God's promise.

"I never prayed to win anything," Teresa says. "I simply believed God's Word that He would meet all my needs, and He has—abundantly more than I could ask or think."

The following March, Teresa flew on an all-expenses-paid trip to Los Angeles where she stayed at the Beverly Hilton. During the awards ceremony, Teresa received a check for $25,000.

Each year since then, Teresa has been flown back to California for an all-expenses-paid educators' retreat.

"I realize now," Teresa says, "that for years before I

even knew about the power of my words, they were working either for or against me. Hundreds of times people mentioned a million-dollar lottery to me and I always confessed that I would take $25,000.

"And for years I told people that my life would really begin at age 45. Sure enough, today I am actively learning the promises that go with being joint heir with Jesus Christ, my children have grown into wonderful adults and I'm engaged to be married to a loving, sensitive man. My life has just begun."

At the awards ceremony Teresa received a gold pin which reads, "To The Educated Belongs The Future."

Teresa Gallman has a personal motto which is even more meaningful: "To The Heirs Belong The Promise."

Update: Teresa is now married to her fiance in the story. The Sawyers (Teresa's new married name) own a bait and tackle business, and Teresa's children have careers of their own. Her son is a painter and has recently been promoted to foreman. Her daughter is a police officer. Teresa still teaches school, special education for 3-, 4- and 5-year-olds.

Teresa has been a Partner with Kenneth Copeland Ministries for 7 years!

From Broken Dreams
To Beautiful Reality

by Melanie Hemry

Worry gnawed Jacqué Furnari's stomach as she drove home through the picturesque Pennsylvania countryside. It had been less than a year since the spring of 1990 when she had moved here to marry Frank. She had come with high hopes, looking forward to a future that shimmered with possibilities. Frank, a plumber with a local company, made a good living at the time, and just a week after they married, Jacqué had opened a craft stand in the Farmer's Market.

The stand had started out as nothing more than a diversion. Jacqué's sales barely covered expenses. But she enjoyed it—and profits really didn't matter.

Then, in 1991, Frank's elbow was seriously injured at work. First, he underwent surgery to remove bone chips. Next followed six months of rehabilitation to regain use of the joint. Soon after he'd returned to work, he and his crew lost their jobs in a company layoff.

As Frank and Jacqué searched the newspaper for job leads they couldn't help but wonder, *What else can happen?* Every time Jacqué turned on the national news, she heard of one financial crisis after another. These problems weren't affecting just the low income and the homeless. They cut right across middle-class America.

"There are computer programmers just one paycheck away from losing their homes," Jacqué's father cautioned. "People get so comfortable in good times, they don't prepare for lean ones."

But Frank and Jacqué *had* prepared. They had a comfortable nest egg in savings. Savings they had dreamed of spending on a home of their own. Now, faced with unemployment and a possible career change at age 40, the American Dream seemed to be crumbling between their fingers.

"I'd always been a worrier," Jacqué admits. "Watching the devastation of families around us gave me more to worry about. The only bright spot in our situation was the teaching of Kenneth and Gloria Copeland.

"Before I moved to Pennsylvania, my Baptist Sunday school teacher had introduced me to their ministry. Now, faced with certain economic ruin, Frank and I started watching their TV broadcast regularly. It seemed that each week, the Copelands gave us the Word we needed to get through.

"One of the first things I learned was to cast my cares on the Lord. It wasn't an easy lesson. For weeks and months I had to give them to Him one worry at a time."

The Furnaris also had to learn to give God their conversation—one *word* at a time. That proved to be even harder. Although they had learned from the Copelands the scriptural power of the spoken word, with a community in crisis, it was only natural to share stories and burdens. It seemed strange and awkward to speak positive words in the midst of such a negative situation.

Then, one day, Jacqué's perspective shifted as childhood memories began to stir in her mind. She recalled early mornings in her grandparents' kitchen, as reliable as the comfortable ticking of the wall clock...*bacon cooking...grandmother rolling out the dough for biscuits...grandfather sitting at the kitchen table reading the Bible aloud.*

As a child, she'd witnessed the scene over and over without thinking much about it. But now, the significance of it dawned on her.

"My grandfather was a farmer who spoke the Word out loud every single morning for years," she says. "And he always seemed to prosper through hard times. Suddenly it hit me: The Holy Spirit had taught him all those years ago to set the course for the day by speaking scripture over it!"

From that moment on, confessing the Word was no longer just a good, scriptural idea to Jacqué. "It was my inheritance!" she says.

Armed with that revelation, Frank and Jacqué Furnari began to radically change their words. Others continued to discuss job shortages, bank failures and economic recession. But the Furnaris said, "Our heavenly Father meets all our needs according to His riches in glory...and our Father is *rich!*"

Since Frank was still unable to find work, he began to help Jacqué transport crafts to the Farmer's Market. Setting up their booth, they discussed the nuggets they had gleaned from the Copelands' most recent teachings.

They were eager to share their growing faith with others too. "We hadn't been trained to witness," says Jacqué, "but that didn't stop us because we had heard Brother Copeland say, 'You don't have to be educated for God to use you. You just have to be available!'"

Frank and Jacqué looked around the bustling market. They were *available* if nothing else! They prayed that the Lord would send people who needed a touch, a prayer or a word of encouragement. That's exactly what He did.

"Strangely, the more I shared my faith with individuals one-on-one, the more calls I received asking me to speak at women's groups. When I was faithful to share in one area, God opened the door for me to share in many places."

As the Furnaris expanded spiritually, their business began to expand too. In the summer of 1991, someone suggested they take their crafts to weekend shows. Frank and Jacqué jumped on the idea and soon they were bustling between Farmer's Market on Tuesday and Friday, and traveling to craft shows on the weekends.

"I had a degree in fashion merchandising, and Frank was a plumber," says Jacqué. "Neither of us knew the first thing about this type of business. We never researched how to do it. I just wandered around the Amish shows looking at lovely quilts and Pennsylvania Dutch artistry. Then I would think about the beautiful crafts I had seen in Texas and other places. And gradually, I began waking up in the morning with new ideas."

One of Jacqué's best ideas was to "import" jewelry from Texas. The jewelry, made by Texas artist Linda Carrigan, was created from pieces of broken china Jacqué purchased on the East Coast. A chipped cup of antique heirloom china might become a brooch and earrings. A broken "Blue Willow" pattern plate could have each scene portrayed in a link bracelet. Customers

> **"My grandfather was a farmer who spoke the Word out loud every single morning for years, and he always seemed to prosper through hard times. Suddenly it hit me: The Holy Spirit had taught him all those years ago to set the course for the day by speaking scripture over it!"**

were so enthusiastic that many special ordered pieces made from their own chipped or broken china.

"Another idea the Lord gave us was for Christian afghans," Jacqué says. "We wanted to sell them so we checked with every manufacturer we knew, but we found only one such afghan. It was a printed message without any picture. Finally, we designed our own. It depicted five scenes from the life of Jesus and carried a scripture to support each scene. Then we ordered a run of 500."

The afghan met with such success that the Furnaris designed another one for Christmas depicting the angelic host around the birth of Jesus.

Having learned the scriptural truth about sowing and reaping, Frank and Jacqué dedicated all their profits from the afghans as seed. In other words, they gave it all away.

As a result, their harvest of blessing grew...and grew...and grew. "When we first took our space at the Farmer's Market, we were out in a field as far from the main traffic as you could get," Jacqué explains. "Most of the old-timers had occupied the prime locations for 20 years. But as God began to bless our work, people asked for us by name and within three years, we were moved to a prime location.

"Eventually, we had to hire people to help with the work. We told them never to worry about sales or numbers, because God would take care of those. Their primary responsibility was to be kind to our customers and *never* say anything negative."

With the market stands flourishing, Jacqué Furnari soon began to dream of opening a permanent shop in one of the quaint little towns in the area. The first time she drove through Strasburg, she knew it was the perfect place.

A Victorian tourist treat, retailers often waited years for commercial space there. Jacqué heard the cautions everywhere she turned. "You'll never get a space in Strasburg!"

Undaunted, Frank and Jacqué prayed in agreement that they *would* get a shop there. Then, each time Jacqué drove through town she said, "Lord, I thank You for giving us a building in Strasburg."

Finally, in March 1994, they heard about a small, vacant shop a half block off Main Street.

"Don't take any space off Main," the doomsayers warned. "Shoppers in Strasburg *never* get off Main Street."

Frank and Jacqué looked at one another and grinned. "We'll *pray* them off Main Street!"

The Furnaris opened their shop in Strasburg on Memorial Day, 1994. From that day forward, the shoppers did indeed leave Main Street to search for unusual buys like Broken China Jewelry. In addition, people from all over the United States began to call and special order their jewelry.

Today, as Jacqué Furnari drives home through the Pennsylvania countryside, she has a lot on her mind, just as she did four years ago. She thinks about filling orders, managing her businesses and sharing Jesus. But one thing she doesn't do is wonder how she and Frank are going to make it.

"Money isn't something we spend time worrying about anymore," Jacqué says, smiling. "After we dedicated our business to the Lord, we didn't stop to calculate the profit until tax season."

Each year the Furnaris prayed and believed God for the increase in their business. At the end of 1991, 1992 and 1993, Frank and Jacqué calculated their total sales and discovered the business had increased by almost 100 percent *each year.* The final figures aren't in yet for 1994, but all predictors indicate another 100-percent increase.

Some might say Frank and Jacqué Furnari's experience has a storybook ending. And, in a way, that's true. Their story is turning out exactly like the Book said it would.

Update: The Furnari's continue to experience God's blessings. They recently closed their store in Strasburg and have opened a new one in Bird In Hand, Pennsylvania.

Frank and Jacqué have been Partners with Kenneth Copeland Ministries for 4 years!

The Bottom Line

by Melanie Hemry

For three years, Dianne Davega had been fighting frantically for her financial life. It had been a desperate battle. She'd done everything she could do.

But it was over.

She just had two more things to take care of...then she'd never have to fight again. Loading her .38-caliber pistol, she looked sadly at her chow, Herman, curled lazily on the bed waiting for his breakfast.

At this moment, Herman and Boss—the two chow dogs she had pampered, spoiled and loved like family for 5½ years—were all that stood between Dianne and death.

Who can I trust to take care of them?

Dianne laid the pistol on the bed next to Herman, then reached over to the nightstand and scratched another name off the list. Wincing at the irony, her mind skimmed the staggering successes she'd enjoyed in years past. Millions of dollars had flowed through her hands—yet now she didn't even have enough money to buy dog food.

Dianne had first arrived in California at age 18, fresh off a farm in Nebraska. Starting her career as a secretary, she'd eventually worked in every phase of the real estate business.

In 1984, she started her own business brokering construction loans. Her fee on the first loan had been $240,000.

Within four years Dianne had brokered $600 million in construction and permanent financing, started a

real estate development company, and set up 11 corporations handling virtually every phase of the real
estate industry.

No longer a simple farm girl, Dianne had moved to
a sprawling home set on 2½ stunning acres. She drove
only one of the five Mercedes she leased, letting her
employees use the others. She employed a full-time
housekeeper-nanny for her two dogs, and traveled
around the world.

Back then, everything Dianne Davega touched had
turned to gold.

Then in late 1988, the once solid savings and loan
industry began to rumble and shake. Dianne desperately hoped it was just a passing tremor. Everything
she did depended on the ability to broker good loans.
If the S & L industry fell, it could topple all of her businesses like a row of dominoes.

"I owned a company that had planned to build a
1 million square-foot wholesale, medical mart on
some land in Nashville. We'd been approved by a
savings and loan in Virginia, but there was a new reg-
ulation that required toxic analysis of the soil.

"I wasn't worried until the sample proved that the
land we were planning to build on had buried gas
tanks under it. It took over a year to clean up the land
and secure the loan. By then the S & L's were beginning to fall. The one that had approved our loan had
been taken over by the FSLIC [Federal Savings & Loan
Insurance Corp.]."

During the same time, late 1988 and 1989, Dianne
was involved in developing 1800 acres in Jackson,
Tennessee. That project included the expense of
rerouting a river. But suddenly the lending sources
were drying up like a lake in a drought.

Dianne worked desperately to secure loans for the multimillion-dollar projects where she was heavily invested.

"After a second lender backed out on the mart in Nashville, a third lender from Canada expressed interest in the project," Dianne recalls. "My lawyers investigated him, the medical company investigated him and the private investor's lawyers investigated him.

"All gave us the same report: he was solid. Furthermore, he was excited about the project and told us the loan was approved. Things began to roll."

Dianne flew to Nashville to meet with the city fathers for final approval of the mart. Before closing, she made the customary good faith deposit of $110,000.

Dianne breathed a sigh of relief. But then things began to go wrong.

The lender postponed closing for a week...then another...and another. *Closing would be on Tuesday. Closing would take place next Wednesday...next month.* Weeks dragged by as Dianne and the other investors hung on to the hope that the next date would close the deal.

"I'll never forget the day I stood in that garage with my homeless friends and realized that regardless of the path we'd each taken to get where we were, the only difference between my car and their shopping cart was my reliance on God."

With each passing day the S & L industry continued to collapse. Dianne finally learned, along with the other investors, that the lender they'd investigated had died. It had been his son—with the same name— who had tried to make the deal and failed.

Dianne Davega was realistic. The deal was

dead. And the S & L industry, as she had known it, no longer existed.

"I spent all of 1991 in court with my various corporations trying to fight bankruptcy," Dianne remembers. "I only handled $2500 that entire year. That was previously pocket change to me. I'd always kept $2-3,000 cash in my wallet. My finances were falling apart, and I had the sense of myself falling...falling...falling. I reached a point where I just wanted to hit bottom so I'd know I couldn't fall anymore.

"By December 1991, I'd lost everything. My CPA showed me that I'd lost millions I'd invested in projects, and more than $100 million in real net worth. The result was less than zero. No cash. No credit. No ability to regroup.

"All my cars were repossessed along with my businesses and inventory. I still had electricity because my home was fenced and no one could get in to turn it off. But I knew I'd lose my home soon.

"I never believed in illness—physical or mental. I never allowed myself to get sick, and even through this loss I never had a headache, an upset stomach or one night of insomnia. I didn't consider myself depressed—just realistic. I'd believed myself to be invincible, and I wasn't. I'd done everything that could be done to salvage something. But nothing had worked and I'd run out of options."

Now, on this crisp, December morning Dianne was ready to end the nightmare with one bullet from her .38. But she couldn't do it until she could think of someone to take care of Herman and Boss. Glancing over at them—one a cuddly, playful companion, the other a stable, strong protector—she thought of their attachment not only to her, but also to each other. The dogs had never spent a single night apart. *I have to think of someone who will keep both of them.* Again, she added a name to the list—then scratched it off.

Frustrated, she flipped on the television—one of five in the house she never watched—and stared at the unfamiliar man on the screen. He was singing a song about God.

God?

Dianne had never thought about God. She'd never considered heaven or hell. But the lyrics of the song tugged at her. *If you can't see God, then it's time you have to believe.*

After the song, the man, Kenneth Copeland, began teaching about God and finances. *God...and finances?* Dianne listened as he preached about Jesus redeeming from poverty those who would believe. He explained God's laws of prosperity.

Dianne had never heard anything like it. He said there was a way out, that Jesus was the Way. At the end of the program Kenneth Copeland led the viewers in a prayer to give their lives to Jesus.

At that moment, Dianne Davega felt like all of time stood still. The words she heard sparked life back into the hope that lay dormant within her. Thoughts of suicide scattered like dry leaves in an autumn wind. She prayed the prayer, asking Jesus into her heart and life. And she promised that whatever she had left would be His.

"I wanted to know more," Dianne says, "so I wrote the Copelands a letter. They flooded me with materials. I devoured everything, and in the process I learned about tithing.

"I knew if I was going to live, I had to have some money. I sold some of my furniture for $2,000. I tithed from the $2,000, then I gave $1,000 to one of my partners. It was the night before Christmas and he was a family man who, like me, had lost everything."

Just as Dianne expected, her house was foreclosed. But something else happened that she would have *never* expected a few months earlier. God sent a man into her life who gave her a car.

"He *gave* me a car! A new Mitsubishi," Dianne explains. "No payments, and best of all, no one could take it away from me. By now I had learned about giving and tithing, and I desperately wanted to give more but I didn't have anything...except clothes. I had *lots* of clothes."

Dianne packed every inch of her new car with clothes and drove to an underground city garage where the homeless strung up blankets for makeshift homes. She didn't see a single person. Parking her car, she stepped out into eerie silence.

"I opened my car and began taking out the clothes," Dianne recalls. "Suddenly dozens of people surrounded me. I couldn't even see where they'd come from. I was terrified that I wouldn't get out alive. Ashamed of my fear, I dumped all the clothes and left.

"But the next week I went back with more clothes. I began going regularly, and finally I started talking to the people and made friends with many of them. I'll never forget the day I stood in that garage with my homeless friends and realized that regardless of the path we'd each taken to get where we were, the only difference between my car and their shopping cart was my reliance on God."

As Dianne continued to act on her growing faith, God continued to move in her circumstances. A friend suddenly offered to let Dianne move into a house he owned at far less than the going rental rate. Then God sent work.

"I did everything in my power to turn my businesses around when they were failing," Dianne says, "but I couldn't do it. Now, God in His graciousness gave me success in helping other people's failing companies."

The days have become months, the months years since that unforgettable Sunday when Dianne gave her life to Jesus. Two years, in fact. During that time, four KCM Believers' Conventions and dozens of books and tapes have undergirded her faith and given her more peace and joy than she has ever known.

These days, Dianne no longer has to fight for finances. She simply fights the good fight of faith.

Is she prospering? Yes. But she'll be the first to tell you that it's not her great job or even the company Mercedes that she prizes now. "Because I have Jesus, I am rich beyond measure."

She no longer looks for answers on the bottom of a profit and loss statement. For Dianne Davega, the Word of God is the bottom line.

Update: Dianne now *owns* the company she was working for at the time her testimony was published—debt free! She also owns two other companies and says business is booming. She continues to minister to the homeless, chasing them down to give them money and talk to them about Jesus. And everyone in her immediate family is now saved. She says God has done so much in recent years, it would take another testimony article to tell it all!

Dianne has been a Partner with Kenneth Copeland Ministries for 4 years!

The Sweet Smell of Success

by Melanie Hemry

Harold Essmaker snapped the lid of his black lunch box shut. Ready for work—at least, as ready as he'd ever be. Stepping outside, he realized the crisp beauty of this sunny Michigan morning should have brought joy to his heart. But it didn't.

Instead, as he looked around him at the ramshackle remnants of his life, bitterness rose in his throat. Turning his back on the travel trailer where he lived with his wife and six children, he sighed heavily and headed toward his dog-eared station wagon.

1975. Was it really only two years ago that he and his family had owned their own home and operated three thriving businesses? It seemed like a lifetime since then.

Harold thought about how, in 1974, his life had begun to unravel. He had been offered the opportunity to join a ministry in another state. A cautious man, he had prayed and sought reliable Christian counsel. In every instance the advice was the same—Do it!

So he and his wife Jean had sold their three businesses (a greenhouse, a Dairy Queen and a country store), moved, and invested all but $10,000 of their savings in the ministry.

Even now, Harold felt a wave of misery when he remembered what had happened. They had been conned—in the Name of Jesus.

When it was over, Harold had returned here to his hometown of Mt. Clemens, Michigan, and taken a job as a hired hand at a local greenhouse. Ironically, it was the same job he'd had 15 years earlier when he was only 25 years old.

Clutching his lunch box, Harold Essmaker left for work. He'd come full circle.

Harold recalls those dismal days: "We lived in the travel trailer for four months. It was located near the greenhouse that my dad had once owned. I was a third-generation rose grower, and just seeing that family greenhouse reminded me of my failures. I was starting over at 40. How would I ever have time to build something substantial enough to pass on to my children?"

Although the sight of the greenhouse saddened Harold, it had the opposite effect on his 9-year-old daughter, Donna. She had been reading a scripture that said God would move a mountain if you had faith and believed when you prayed. The solution to her dad's problems seemed simple to her young mind. He needed a business. The greenhouse her grandpa used to own would do nicely.

So what if the business wasn't for sale and her parents were almost broke? She figured a greenhouse was a lot easier for God to move than a mountain. So, each morning as she stood at the end of their driveway waiting for the school bus, she would turn toward that greenhouse and speak quietly to it, *"Mountain be removed."*

Without saying a word about it to any member of her family, Donna repeated her prayer each morning for six months.

In January the announcement was made. The greenhouse was for sale. That night Donna dressed for bed, catching bits and pieces of her parents' conversation. "But the down payment..." "...wipe out the last of our savings." "If there's a chance..." "Let's pray..."

Smiling into her pillow, Donna went to sleep.

Within weeks the sale was finalized. The Essmakers were back in business. Their savings depleted, Harold and Jean worked long hours trying to turn a profit. Like any business, cultivating roses required operating capital. Harold and Jean didn't have any.

"By the end of our first year in business," Harold explains, "I thought I'd have to sell the greenhouse just to survive. I couldn't figure out why everything kept going wrong for me. Jean and I tithed and were faithful to give when directed."

Threading his way through rows of roses, Harold paced through the greenhouse and prayed, "Lord, should I sell it?" In answer, a familiar, quiet voice spoke up inside Harold's heart, *Someday people from around the world will come here to ask you for the secrets to your success.*

Harold knew that voice well. It was the voice of the Holy Spirit. But he was puzzled.

This greenhouse was the smallest in all of Michigan. He couldn't imagine people coming here to ask how he grew his roses. Had he imagined those words? Back in his office, Harold thumbed through his Bible, seeking wisdom.

He found what he was looking for in Malachi 3:10: *"Bring ye all the tithes into the storehouse, that there may be meat in mine house, and prove me now herewith, saith the Lord of hosts, if I will not open you the windows of heaven, and pour you out a blessing, that there shall not be room enough to receive it."*

Harold's heart quickened as he read the scripture. He definitely needed the windows of heaven to open. But it was the next verse that convinced him not to sell the greenhouse.

"And I will rebuke the devourer for your sakes, and he shall not destroy the fruits of your ground; neither shall your vine cast her fruit before the time in the field...And all nations shall call you blessed: for ye shall be a delightsome land...."

Crops...vines...all nations.... Could God really be saying that *his* crops—roses—would prosper so much that people actually would come from all over the world? Harold wasn't sure, but he knew one thing. He wasn't going to sell.

"I realized God really wanted me to prosper," Harold says, "but there was something about tithing that I didn't understand. Finally, one day I was praying and the Lord spoke again. He said, *You haven't expected to receive My blessings in response to your tithing. So when those blessings come, you let them slip right past you."*

"Each season," says Harold, "the Lord began telling us what variety of roses to choose, as well as when and how fast to make a change. Following His lead, we developed an edge on the market."

Soon after that, Harold and Jean received a phone call from a man they knew in northern Michigan. He said the Lord had told him to send the Essmakers $220. Two hundred for them to spend, he explained, and $20 to be tithed.

With six children to care for, there was always a need for extra money in the Essmaker household, but Harold and Jean felt this money was different. God had something special in mind for it. Tithing the $20, they prayed for His direction on the $200.

That direction came through a woman in their

church who loaned the Essmakers two tapes by Kenneth Copeland. Harold had never heard of Kenneth Copeland and wasn't too interested but, out of courtesy, he listened to them.

A stickler for accuracy where the Word was concerned, Harold hadn't listened to the tapes long before he said, "No! That's not right!" Stopping the tape, he looked up the scripture Brother Copeland had quoted and studied it in context. It was right!

"I'd been raised in the Catholic church," Harold explains. "Jean and I were born again in 1966, sitting in front of our television watching a televangelist. I believed the Bible was the final authority, but I'd never heard it taught like Brother Copeland taught it.

"It took me two weeks to finish the two tapes," Harold recalls. "By the time I got through them, I'd worn out the on-off switch on the tape player. But I'd learned enough to know there was light at the end of my financial tunnel. And I was determined to get out!"

The next day, Jean called Kenneth Copeland Ministries to request more tapes and discovered the ministry offered an entire tape series designed for beginners like the Essmakers. Tentatively, she asked the price. The set cost $200—the exact amount of the gift they'd received. Without hesitation, Jean and Harold ordered the entire set.

A year later, they mailed a $600 check to KCM to order more tapes. They took all their tapes to the greenhouse and set up a lending library.

"Our employees listen to the tapes at work," Jean explains. "The customers hear preaching when they come into the greenhouse. In the summer, neighbors in their yards hear the teaching. Our roses are saturated with the Word!"

That Word immediately began to give the Essmakers an edge in the rose industry. In a business that is famous for its quick changes, where varieties come and go in a season and it's anyone's guess what variety will be in demand each year, Harold and Jean were a step ahead of the rest. "Each season," says Harold, "the Lord began telling us what variety of roses to choose, as well as when and how fast to make a change. Following His lead, we developed an edge on the market."

That wasn't the only thing the Lord taught them, either. He led them to put in a lighting system despite the fact that other growers insisted such systems were too expensive in their part of the country. Then He directed them to put in a fog system. Others in the industry ridiculed that, too.

"It's been my experience that following the Word brings rejection," Harold admits. "I've learned to let go of bitterness and always do whatever the Lord says to do."

In addition to the equipment changes, the Essmakers made changes in how they treated their employees. Since the Bible clearly states that a workman is worthy of his hire, Harold and Jean began paying their employees some of the highest wages in the industry for comparable positions—even though their greenhouse is the smallest in their state. By natural reasoning, such a step should have been a fatal blow to their profit margin. But it wasn't. Instead, the more the Essmakers aligned their business with the Word, the more their profit margin crept upward.

Then the summer of 1991 hit the rose industry with a fierce blow. Recession. Even the word struck fear in rose growers. After all, roses were a luxury item. When greenhouses in the Michigan area began cutting expenses to survive the recession, they were struck with a second blow. Heat. A 90-degree heat that reduced a rose head to half its normal size and left leaves and stems sickened and weak.

But, strangely enough, that killing heat seemed to lose its power at the Essmakers' greenhouse.

Each day as they went to cut their roses, they found the same inexplicable thing. Their rose heads were full and perfect. The stems strong and straight. In fact, for five straight months—before, during and after the summer of 1991—the Essmakers' profit margin broke every record. In the midst of recession and heat, their income was 33 percent higher than at any other time in the history of the greenhouse.

Today, Harold Essmaker is 58 years old. His six children are grown. He and Jean are prosperous beyond their dreams.

Their fog and lighting systems have set the standard in the industry. They could retire and live comfortably in a resort town. But they don't. Harold likes to be on hand when the huge Greyhound buses arrive with tours from the national association, Roses Incorporated.

Rose experts from all over the United States, France and the Netherlands have traveled to Mt. Clemens to tour Michigan's smallest greenhouse. Invariably, they pull Harold Essmaker aside and ask the same question, "What's the secret of your success with roses?"

Harold answers them with intricate details about lighting, fogging, fertilizing and cutting the roses. But first, he tells them the simple, straightforward truth.

"You see," he explains, "the Lord knows how to grow roses because He created them...I just ask Him."

Update: When Harold updated us on his and Jean's lives, he shared the following testimony of God's goodness:

"My wife of 40 years, Jean, suddenly went to be with Jesus 'in the twinkling of an eye' without any warning. She looked into Jesus' face and her own face reflected a beauty I had never seen, and I knew that what we had believed and lived was true. I knew that I knew, that what I knew, I really knew. Psalm 139:16, *'The pages of the book of our lives are written before they begin to be (my translation).'* Jean left as she had lived, and our God honored her totally. My spiritual heart is, and has been, quiet and settled and blessing my heavenly Father for His love. My human heart has had a much harder time...."

In January of 1995, Harold sold his business to his son, and he is now retired, looking for his Lord's call to work.

Harold (and Jean) has been a Partner with Kenneth Copeland Ministries for 19 years!

With Long Life
He Satisfies Them

by Melanie Hemry

Terrel Davis opened the door for his wife Audrey, and they stepped into the crowded room. Audrey rushed off to hug members of the congregation while Terrel opened his Bible. The pages were dog-eared and worn, marked by years of diligent use. He fingered the scripture passage he would share, letting the familiar words saturate his heart and mind.

Terrel opened the service with prayer, praise and worship. Even after 10 years of ministering here at Whispering Pines Nursing Home, the opportunity always tugged at Terrel's heart. Bowing his head, he thanked God for entrusting these souls to his care.

Terrel looked down at his hands, wrinkled and calloused from years of hard work. At 83 years of age, Terrel Davis had few illusions. Apart from the grace of God's Word in his life, he might be sitting in this room anxiously awaiting a touch from God instead of being the one to offer it.

Terrel and Audrey had seen the golden years turn brass for many people after the age of retirement. Indeed, for most folk in their 80s and beyond, health problems, loneliness and creeping poverty were commonplace.

Yet at a time when the world system says you must decrease, the Davises had managed to increase. How? They had simply trusted God to be faithful to His Word. They believed that just as Psalm 91 said, He would satisfy them with long life and show them His salvation in every area.

Sure enough, He had. In fact, sometimes it seemed that for the Davises, retirement had marked the beginning of their most productive years.

"When I retired from the Bossier Parish Highway Department at age 65," Terrel says, "the change in our routine was unsettling. Audrey wasn't sure what she'd do with me under foot all day.

"Spiritually, my name was on the Methodist Church rolls, but I belonged to Jesus Christ. I'd never learned the books of the Bible, and I couldn't find my way around in one at all. Still, I knew the gospel and I wasn't ashamed to spread it."

On Christmas, before Terrel retired in 1974, their daughter, Lanette Miles and her husband Larry, gave them a tape player and three sets of tapes by a young minister named Kenneth Copeland.

The topic of those tapes perked Terrel's interest. "Revelation knowledge" sounded good to him. He set up the tape player and began to listen. The teaching he heard was different than anything he'd heard before. It sounded good, but was it *right?*

He stopped the tape, pulled out his Bible and began the laborious task of finding the scripture reference. Finally, he turned to the index and looked up the page number of each book. Over and over again, Terrel turned the pages of his Bible, marking a new road map to faith.

"I looked up every scripture Brother Copeland mentioned in those tapes," Terrel recalls. "It didn't happen fast, but over time I consumed those tapes and in the process I learned the books of the Bible. I bought the first study Bible Kenneth Copeland ever published, and I've bought two more since then."

In the following years, Terrel continued to listen to

more teachings by Kenneth Copeland, and in January 1977, Terrel and Audrey went to Texarkana, Arkansas, to hear the Copelands in person.

"Up till that point," Terrel says, "I'd never really heard the law of prosperity taught from the Bible. God had directed me to get out of debt back in the '50s when I'd worked for Stanley Products Company, and eventually I'd gotten us on a cash basis. But I still hadn't gotten ahead.

"That night in Texarkana, Brother Copeland said if anyone wanted to support his ministry they could give the price of a pair of tennis shoes, which was $12.50 back then. Audrey and I talked it over. We liked this young couple and wanted to be a part of what they were doing. So we gave $15 that day.

"We've given something every month since then. We helped them buy the land at Eagle Mountain, and we've reaped rich dividends on that investment."

It's true. The Davis' lifestyle of steady faith and love for God has paid rich dividends in every way. So rich that Terrel—who had to quit school in the eighth grade to help support his family through the Great Depression—has prospered more in his retirement years than he did when he worked eight hours a day.

"God gave us wisdom about when to sell land, when to retain mineral rights and where to plant financial seed," Terrel explains. "I sat in my rocking chair and watched God multiply my finances. In 1987, we bought a brand-new Oldsmobile 98...and paid cash. The day I retired I only had about $1500 in the bank, now it has grown to over a hundredfold."

The Davises have prospered spiritually, too. In 1982, Terrel and Audrey's Sunday school teacher began pleading for volunteers to lead services at a nursing home. No one was interested.

"I kept thinking that Terrel and I should lead those services," Audrey remembers, "but I didn't say anything until Terrel mentioned it to me. So on the second Sunday in July 1982 we showed up at the Whispering Pines Nursing Home.

"People who could walk joined us, and nurses brought others in wheelchairs. We prayed that the Lord would lead the service. Afterward, we closed with the Lord's Prayer. I was amazed that only a handful of people knew it. Now they are eager to join us as we close each service with the Lord's Prayer."

The response to the Davis' ministry was so overwhelming, they committed to lead the services every Sunday.

"God blesses everything His children do," Audrey says, "and that's something in itself—to be our age, and have Him call us children."

The Davises *do* still enjoy life with a delightfully childlike enthusiasm. For example, about 10 years ago, their hometown, Plain Dealing, Louisiana, built a golf course. Their four children encouraged Terrel and Audrey to join the country club and take up golf. "We decided to do just that," Audrey says, "but we made a commitment to our Lord that we would not play on Sundays."

"God so blessed us," Terrel says, "that when we play scrambles, it's common to hear someone on the sidelines point to us and say, 'See those folks? Watch them, because one of them is gonna place.'

"It's true, we win a lot. We're a two-golf cart family now!"

Of course, the Davis' journey of faith hasn't been without trial. On February 9, 1990, Terrel woke at 5 a.m. with chest pain. Audrey followed the ambulance's flashing lights and cried out to God, "Lord, I need You now!" And He was there.

"I was home within a week," Terrel says. "Eight men that we knew had heart attacks at about that same time. I'm the only one they didn't carry to the cemetery."

The reason is clear. Terrel and Audrey knew their covenant rights. And they knew the Lord wasn't finished with them yet.

Now at ages 83 and 79, they are much older than many of the people they minister to at the nursing home. But then age is no problem. They have faith in the God Who promised *with long life will I satisfy them and show them My salvation.*

Update: Terrel, now 86, and Audrey, now 82, still visit the Whispering Pines Nursing Home every Sunday morning. The second Sunday in July of 1995 began their 14th year of ministry there.

Terrel and Audrey have been Partners with Kenneth Copeland Ministries for 19 years!

CHAPTER 5

Testimonies of Deliverance

*"And the Lord shall help them, and deliver them:
he shall deliver them from the wicked,
and save them, because they trust in him."*

Psalm 37:40

Help Me, God!
I'll Do *Anything!*

by Melanie Hemry

Alan Crider looked over the balcony to the dance floor below. "Let's go," his friends called, waving to him.

"I'll meet you downstairs!" Alan answered. The combination of drugs and alcohol in his system suddenly filled him with a sense of power. *I don't have to take the stairs,* he reasoned. *I can fly.*

Moments later, he leapt from the balcony—waving his arms gracefully—before crashing to the floor below. His friends dragged his crumpled body to a car, then left him in an apartment alone and unconscious.

Eighteen hours later, Alan opened his eyes to blinding pain, a broken wrist and the sickening realization of just how far he'd really fallen in life.

A few short years ago he'd been one of the youngest men promoted to Regional Sales Manager for a national carpet company. With a sales staff of 21, his territory had included 17 states.

It hadn't been his job performance that cost him his position. It had been chronic lying—a behavior necessary to cover his serious drinking problem.

Since then, his life had spiraled downward. He drank or gambled away the money he earned. He was running numbers at the local bars. He "dated" other women while his wife sat at home. His marriage was terminal, and his children hardly knew him.

Wincing in pain, Alan struggled to his feet, guarding his throbbing wrist. He felt trapped inside his own lifestyle and he had no idea how to change it. *Somebody help me!* he cried silently. But there was no answer.

Two months later, Alan was staying with a friend when he discovered a Gideon Bible. Grabbing a six-pack of beer from the refrigerator, he popped a can open and dropped on the sofa to read. He thumbed through the Bible and stopped at the book of Daniel.

For the next seven hours, Alan read stories he'd never heard. Stories about Daniel in the lions' den, and the three Hebrews that walked out of a fire untouched. When he read about the kingdoms represented in a statue with ten iron toes, he *knew* those toes represented the iron curtain and communism.

This book is true!

He lay the Bible aside that night a broken man. Weeping, he cried out to God, "I didn't know! I didn't know! I never would have lived my life this way if I'd known!"

"I still wasn't sure what to do," Alan remembers. "I knew the Bible was true, and there was a God. I had never heard about Jesus. I didn't know there was a plan of salvation. I figured the thing to do was go to church.

"For the next six months, my wife, Terri, and I attended a denominational church. But somehow I never heard about Jesus. I tried to change myself—to give up alcohol, drugs and women—but it never lasted.

Alan slid onto a bar stool and ordered two martinis. Frustration rose like bile in his throat. He *wanted* to live a Christian life, but *how?* Soon, the alcohol loosened his tongue, and he found himself telling the man sitting beside him the whole story—his addictions, his assurance that the Bible was true and his inability to live a Christian life.

"There's a guy downtown preaching tonight," the man said. "My sister's real big on this stuff, and she's going. He might have the answers you want. Maybe you should go."

Alan left the bar nine martinis later and drove around for 45 minutes. He didn't want to be seen at some religious meeting. But he couldn't help wondering, *What if this man does have the answers I need?* Finally, he hid his car behind another nearby bar and slipped into the convention center.

An usher met him in the lobby. "Brother," he said, "there's a place for you right down front."

"I don't want to sit in front," Alan argued. The usher lifted his hand and signaled another man. Moments later, they led Alan to his chair—front row, third seat.

"The singing stopped soon after that," Alan remembers. "Kenneth Copeland walked out. I looked up and saw right into his eyes. There was an awesome presence about him. He started speaking in a language I'd never heard. I thought, *My God, what's going on here?"*

Kenneth Copeland finished the message in tongues and gave the interpretation. Then he began to preach. For the first time in his life, Alan Crider heard about Jesus and His death on the cross for our sins. He listened awe-struck to this man describe the power of God available to overcome sin through the new birth and the Baptism in the Holy Spirit.

"I prayed the sinner's prayer," Alan recalls. "Then when they prayed for people who wanted to be baptized in the Holy Spirit, I raised my hands toward heaven and *screamed*, 'God, I need You! Help me! I'll do anything!'"

Alan stepped into the lobby after the service and called Terri. "I'm born again!" he announced.

"Yeah...right." Terri said. She'd heard so many lies out of his mouth she didn't believe much of anything her husband said.

But over the next few weeks and months, Terri not only began to believe her husband, she followed his lead, giving her own life to Jesus and receiving the Baptism in the Holy Spirit. For no matter how skeptical she tried to be, she simply couldn't deny the dramatic changes in Alan.

He stopped drinking. He didn't use drugs. He was faithful to her. Over and over she caught him telling the *truth*. He stopped partying. He became compassionate. He took responsibility for the children. He even paid the bills—no small feat considering how severely Alan had damaged his career.

> **Alan opened his eyes to blinding pain, a broken wrist and the sickening realization of just how far he'd really fallen in life.**

"I lost my job right after I was saved," Alan explains. "No one would give me work. One man told me straight out that I'd ruined my reputation in the carpet business. We didn't have *anything*, but we'd heard Brother Copeland say God didn't want His children broke. Through his teachings we'd learned the principle of sowing and reaping. So we knew that to increase we needed to plant whatever we had in abundance."

Alan looked around the house. They didn't have anything in abundance—except lack. *Look out the back window*, the Lord said. Alan walked over to the window and looked out. There, in the back yard, was the one and only thing they had in abundance: zucchini. It was growing everywhere!

"We started giving away zucchini," Alan says. "We

put zucchini in unlocked cars in the church parking lot. We chopped zucchini, boiled zucchini, fried zucchini, made zucchini bread and zucchini casserole. After a while, people started locking their cars."

About a month after they started planting zucchini, God urged a man to give Alan another chance in the carpet business. He would work on straight commission.

"I learned how to get a harvest," Alan says. "Every time I showed someone a carpet sample—it didn't matter if they bought it or not—I prayed. 'Lord,' I'd say, 'that's my seed. I plant it in faith.'"

Five months later, that seed sprouted. Alan's first check: $3,748. Alan and Terri paid their obligations and gave $714 to the Methodist church to feed the needy.

Following the biblical principles they'd learned, Alan and Terri watched their harvest grow. That first year Alan made $50,000 on straight commission. The next year he made $70,000. Soon Alan's income was ranging between $125,000 to $155,000.

"We went from one television to five," Terri recalls. "From one car to three. We custom built our dream home on three acres. The house had scriptures made into the foundation, over the windows and doorposts. We included a specially designed prayer closet."

Each time they heard Kenneth and Gloria teach something, they implemented it in their lives. When Gloria taught the series titled *Walk in the Spirit*, she mentioned that the spiritual revelation from praying in tongues an hour each day had changed her life.

"I'm going to dedicate my life," Alan declared, "to praying in tongues for an hour every day, and studying the Word of God for an hour a day."

When Kenneth taught a series on *Intercessory Prayer*,

they started praying for their city and the nation as he taught.

During those times of prayer, the Lord confirmed to both Alan and Terri that He was calling them to start a church. They held the first service in their home on March 3, 1988. A year later, they sold their home to pay off their debts and rented a 3600-square-foot storefront building to use as a church.

"We started taking evangelism teams, praise and worship teams, and free meals to the inner city ghetto," Alan explains. "On one of our first crusades, we cooked 5,000 pieces of chicken, had praise and worship, and 40 evangelism teams. We won 750 souls to the Lord that day.

"Afterward, a single mother of three came up to me and asked how she could get out of the ghetto. We discussed her situation, and I didn't have any answers for her. I knew then that what we were doing wasn't enough."

Today, the 800-member congregation of River of L.I.F.E. Church has gone the extra mile to get people not only off the path toward destruction, but onto the road to recovery.

They are still called to go into ghettos and hold crusades, but they also own two thrift stores, and the Criders operate a tire store and furniture store. Why would a pastor want to operate businesses?

"So that when we lead someone to the Lord and they ask how to get off the street, or out of the ghetto, we have an answer. We can employ new converts in the businesses and at the church while they're being discipled. We also offer Life Line (a counseling service that covers marriage, legal, financial issues, alcohol or drug abuse), and housing for these new believers while they work to become financially and spiritually stable."

It has been 18 years now since Alan Crider promised that he would do anything if God would only help him. During those years, he and Terri have been blessed beyond their wildest dreams. Yet even so, they're still keeping their end of that bargain.

And the miraculous changes in the lives that surround them are undeniable proof that God is still keeping His.

Update: Alan and Terri continue to pastor River of L.I.F.E. Church, and along with several other churches, made possible the 1995 Chattanooga Victory Campaign.

Alan and Terri have been Partners with Kenneth Copeland Ministries for 16 years!

In the Ranks
of a Royal Army

"There's somebody here who has a fear of death, and God wants to deliver you."

When Janet heard that statement, she knew it was meant for her.

A regular Valium user who had been suffering from agoraphobia (a fear of open spaces) for two years, Janet Wood was desperate for a way out of the terror that had often held her captive in her Warminster, England, home.

Her husband, Stephen, sat beside her burdened with fear and the misery of a rocky marriage. Both of them knew they needed to make changes in their lives. But, until they heard those startling, prophetic words, they didn't even know how to begin.

Four years have passed since that night, but memories of it are still clear in Stephen's mind. "I experienced the love of God as soon as I walked through that door," says Stephen. "There was something in that room—in that house—that I'd been missing all my life."

"I saw these people with their hands in the air, praising God and singing in this foreign language," adds Janet. "I knew that what they had, I needed."

Initially, the Woods had been reluctant to attend that first Kenneth Copeland videotape meeting. But the love and warmth expressed by the Canadian neighbors who invited them (and who had been praying for them for 18 months) were tough to refuse.

And, once there, they both reached out for the help they had needed for so long.

"I asked the group to pray for me, and after the prayer I knew I was delivered and set free from fear—delivered from agoraphobia," Janet says.

"Nobody prayed with me. Nobody laid hands on me. I just knew that I had received Jesus that night," Stephen adds. "When we went home that evening, I felt lighter, much happier, more joyful and much more peaceful. And from that day on, we just prayed and read the Word and studied."

Before the Woods left the videotape meeting that night, they knew their lives had been changed. But what they didn't realize was just how drastic and far-reaching that change would be.

Within six months, Stephen, a warrant officer in the British Army, was transferred to Germany. There the couple decided to become KCM Covenant Partners and video ministers themselves.

"We knew it was God's will," says Janet. "If it hadn't been for Kenneth's tapes—both audio and video—we would have fallen apart over there," Stephen said. "It was just such a spiritual desert in Germany."

Even in that spiritual desert, the videotapes had a profound impact on many the Woods came in contact with. Day by day they saw people's lives change, just as theirs had. Being a part of that process was an exciting opportunity. But it didn't come without paying a price. Stephen and Janet were sharply criticized by many there who were opposed to the faith message they brought. At one point, two officers even threatened to get them sent out of Germany within 24 hours if they didn't stop laying hands on people, praying for deliverance and healing.

But the Woods absolutely refused to compromise.

"We WERE persecuted, but we know our God is true," Janet says. "[And we told the Lord] we would never stop showing Copeland videos [and ministering] until HE told us."

Today the Woods are back in their hometown of Warminster. The fear and misery that brought them to that first KCM videotape meeting four years ago have long since been replaced by the faith and joy of the Lord. But the Woods aren't content to simply sit back and count their own blessings. They've been compelled to pass them along to others.

That's why both of them are now full-time ministers of the gospel. On September 7, 1995, these Covenant Partners began a new church—Foundation Christian Fellowship Warminster—in their hometown of nearly 15,000.

And though Stephen has retired from the British service, he and Janet have joined the ranks of another, more powerful army. "The Lord is raising up a Gideon's army in England—a special core of His army that's specially trained to do tasks that other troops aren't trained for," explains Janet. "And He's raising up those people who are totally committed, whose lives are sold out to God...And if we'll only listen, He'll give us our orders and train us up."

Covenant Partners Janet and Stephen Wood are two of those specially trained spiritual soldiers. And now that they've received their orders, they're marching forward as mighty conquerors, claiming their city and country for the Lord.

Update: Since their testimony was first published, Stephen and Janet have continued to minister through Foundation Christian Fellowship. They have literally seen hundreds of lives changed as they have reached out with the freedom of God's Word.

Now He Weeps for Joy

by Melanie Hemry

Sunday morning, as the sanctuary of Victory Christian Center swelled with strains of "Hosanna," Steve Marvel reached for his wife Crys' hand. Steve had plenty to be grateful for: born again and Spirit filled, he had a wonderful wife, a successful career, a nice car and a home with a pool. He had it all.

Yet, on that lovely Sunday morning, Steve Marvel was weeping.

No one knew why. Crys didn't know. His pastor didn't know. His friend didn't know. Only God knew the sad secret Steve struggled to conceal.

Nestled in the breast pocket of his well-cut suit—next to his heart—was a prescription bottle of amphetamines. *Speed.* Exhausted after praise and worship, Steve slipped out to the bathroom. Behind locked doors, he opened the bottle and slipped some of the shiny, death-black capsules into his hand.

Swallowing half a capsule, Steve waited for the familiar rush. Now energy surged through his body. He returned to the sanctuary riding high on the euphoric confidence of the chemical...and slid confidently back into his seat.

To others, mixing a worship service with a drug-induced high might have seemed bizarre. But to Steve it was simply a matter of survival. He was, in fact, a believer and a drug addict. So no matter how paradoxical his behavior seemed, he was locked into repeating it—again and again.

"I didn't become a Christian until I was 25," Steve

says, recalling the progression of events that led up to that terrible time. "I'd had a problem with alcohol before I committed my life to Christ, and obviously, the devil decided to use that to bring me down because after I was born again the addiction accelerated at a terrifying pace. I repented and cried to God, but during physical withdrawal, I'd ultimately take another drink. Crys had no idea I was drinking. I had alcohol hidden under the sofa, in the cabinet of an antique record player, and in the weeds behind my house."

Steve began to gain weight as his drinking increased. When he finally tipped the scales at 250 pounds, he went to the doctor for help.

"My doctor prescribed amphetamines to help me lose weight," Steve remembers. "And I did lose weight the first month, but I quickly became addicted. I was under conviction about my drinking and miserable about my weight. The speed gave me a sense of well-being. The world's kind of peace.

"It's hard to explain, but the drug developed a personality of its own. At first, I kept the bottle in my glove compartment. As a traveling salesman, I spent hours each day in my car. Eventually, I began to worry that the heat might hurt the capsules, so I locked them in my briefcase and carried it with me. Then I developed this horrible fear: What if someone stole my briefcase!

"That's when I transferred them to my breast pocket. I could feel them there and know they were safe. But when I was driving my car, I'd get restless because I couldn't *see* them. Finally, I'd put the bottle on the dash."

Taking speed as many as four times a day, Steve's life became a carnival ride gone awry. After "speeding" all day, he'd drink alcohol in the evening to mellow out, then take barbiturates to sleep. When the barbiturates wore off at three in the morning, Steve would stumble barefoot through the frigid winter darkness outside to his stash of alcohol. Next day, he'd begin the cycle again.

Even though he couldn't seem to lay hold of the victory that belonged to him as a believer, Steve stubbornly refused to give up on it. "I even believed I could study the Bible best on speed," says Steve. "And I was faithful in church attendance, although I was too drugged to grasp much. My only link with spiritual reality was the hours I spent driving in my car listening to cassette tapes by Kenneth and Gloria Copeland. I remember being high on drugs, driving, listening to tapes, and taking notes at the same time. Over the years, I bought almost every tape the Copelands offered."

> **"God, I've been a Christian nine years. My trunk's full of booze. I'm close to losing my family. What are You going to do?"**

Why was he so drawn to the Copelands?

"I was driving down the interstate one day when I heard Kenneth tell about how he used to drink, smoke a bathtub full of cigarettes, sing in clubs, and fight," he explains. *"Kenneth Copeland!* I started sobbing when I heard that because suddenly I saw a glimmer of hope. Even in my mental state, I knew God was no respecter of persons. If Kenneth Copeland could get delivered of those things, I could get delivered too. I thought if I listened to him long enough, I'd find out *how.*"

The problem was, Steve didn't have that long to wait. Although for a while, his traveling had enabled him to hide his habit, his drinking was quickly catching up with him.

The crisis came one day as he and his family were preparing to leave on vacation. Steve passed out on the floor, right in front of Crys. Threatening to leave Steve, Crys called the church pastor for help.

"After that, a lying spirit came on me," Steve recalls, "and I became a master of deception. I convinced Crys I'd stopped drinking. She didn't know about the drugs, so she came back to me. I was terrified she'd find out about the amphetamines."

But that terror was not enough to make Steve give them up. The drug had too powerful a hold on him. When he was using it, he felt invincible.

He wasn't, however. And the truth of that soon began to dawn on him. One evening, for instance, when he was on a business trip, Steve pulled into a filling station in Missouri at 7 o'clock to map out his traveling strategy and decide which road to take. Later he became aware of papers, filled with strategies, strewn across the car seat. It was 9 p.m. Unaware of time, he'd been sitting in the car—engine running—for two hours trying to make a decision.

"It was a nightmare," Steve recalls. "I knew I was digging my own grave—pill by pill. I made a decision to stop the speed, and God helped me stay off for almost a year. But my wounded spirit hadn't healed, and eventually, I started back. When I took the drug again, my addiction was seven times worse than before."

In 1986, Steve bought Kenneth Copeland's tape series *Developing Friendship With God.* Deep in his spirit, Steve knew that the answer to his problems would be found in those tapes. For the next year, while he continued his roller coaster of drugs and alcohol, Steve listened to the tapes literally hundreds of times.

"I listened to them so often that they got down into my spirit. I began to see God as my daddy. My prayers changed when I learned to crawl into His lap and press into Him. Many times over 10 months, whether I was high on speed or coming down on alcohol, I spoke the same confession out loud. *'According to the Word of God, I have power over drugs and alcohol. Greater is He that is in me than he that is in the world. I am slim. I am healthy. I am no longer addicted. I sleep the whole night long.'*"

On October 31, 1987, Crys woke unexpectedly and found Steve drinking a margarita. She expressed no anger. Made no threats. She simply went back to bed. Steve stood outside the room and listened to her uncontrollable sobbing. Then she prayed.

The sound of Crys' sobs followed Steve the next week. Making a faith stand, Steve called his physician. "I told him I was addicted and needed help," Steve remembers. "I made him promise to never give me another prescription again. No matter what I did."

Two weeks later, on Saturday night, Steve lay in bed while Crys slept. Although he'd gone two weeks without drugs, he'd just made an emergency run to the liquor store to buy what he'd need to make it through Sunday: three six-packs of six point beer and a pint of vodka.

Sorrow welled up in Steve, and he began to weep. What good was it to quit amphetamines if alcohol continued to control his life? Despairing of ever being free, he whispered, "God, I've been a Christian nine years. My trunk's full of booze. I'm close to losing my family. What are You going to do?"

The answer was swift and clear. *Nothing. I love you even more than you love your own son. But I've done all I can do. What are you going to do?*

"Well...I won't take a drink to go to sleep tonight."

Okay, that sounds good.

"But what about when I wake up at 3 a.m.?"

We'll talk about it then. Good night.

Steve fell asleep at 11:05 that night. At 7 a.m. he woke, healed and delivered from alcohol. "It was the first time in years that I'd slept without drugs or alcohol. I never experienced withdrawal, and I never wanted another drink. Later I went through the act of deliverance to make sure every door was closed to the devil."

A month later Steve Marvel was still sober...and he *still* weighed 250 pounds. Sitting in a pizza parlor with a huge pizza in front of him, he bowed his head and prayed, "God, what are You going to do about the way I look?"

The answer was swift and familiar. *I've done everything that I can do. What are you going to do?*

"Well...I could fast this piece of pizza."

Okay. That sounds good.

One year later, Steve weighed 179 pounds.

It's been three years since Steve has taken a drug or had a drink. When he goes to church now, he goes with nothing to hide. There are still times when he weeps during worship, but these days his tears are very different from those he used to cry. Now he weeps for joy.

Steven has been a Partner with Kenneth Copeland Ministries for 17 years!

Free at Last

by Melanie Hemry

Lisa King sank into an overstuffed chair at the sorority where she lived in Raleigh, North Carolina. A sophomore at North Carolina State University, Lisa seemed to have it all.

She'd been accepted into the best sorority on campus. She excelled academically. A natural athlete, Lisa's room at home was cluttered with trophies and awards. She'd been a star basketball player since fifth grade. She'd been voted most valuable dancer in her ballet troupe. An excellent swimmer, she'd excelled on the summer swim team.

Over the years, she had grown used to the sound of cheering crowds. But in her own private battle, Lisa had lost and there was no applause.

With time to spare between classes, Lisa clicked on the television set. Flipping through the channels, she stopped, mesmerized by one program. Leaning forward, she listened intently to every word.

When the program ended, she pressed the remote control and sat staring at a blank screen. She couldn't believe it. She'd stumbled onto *the answer!* Oprah Winfrey, looking slim and gorgeous, had just shared the secret of her weight loss success: Optifast. Lisa celebrated her discovery with a pizza for lunch—double cheese.

"I could date the beginning of my eating disorder to age 13," Lisa says. "Back then, I had a slender, athletic body. But I began noticing other girls with bulging bodies and I didn't want that to happen to mine.

"Instead of continuing the eating and exercising that had won me a good figure in the first place, I tried to prevent future problems by skipping meals and 'saving' calories for after school. Sometimes I'd eat a pitiful few calories at a meal just so I could justify the candy bar I wanted later.

"By the following year, my sophomore year in high school, my 'dieting' had reaped results. I had gained so much weight I had to wear shorts and T-shirts over my leotard at dance class. It was my worst fear come true."

During her junior year, Lisa continued her "diet" and gained 50 pounds. That summer she went on the 21 Day Diet and lost down to 130 pounds, which was still heavy for her small frame. By Lisa's senior year, there were two things she wanted desperately: to have a boyfriend, and to be skinny.

"I started my senior year slender enough to attract attention," Lisa remembers. "Soon I had a new boyfriend and life was wonderful. When that relationship ended, I ate my way through my sorrow. It took years before I realized the pattern: lose weight, date new boyfriend, break up, feel sad, get fat."

Lisa started college overweight. And with each trip to the school cafeteria, her food addiction revealed itself further. She found herself eating twice as much as others: two doughnuts, two bagels, two bowls of cereal. By the first break, she'd gained 30 pounds. Tipping the scales at 180, Lisa knew she'd have to do something drastic. That's when she saw Oprah and discovered the Optifast solution.

"An Optifast group met in Charlotte, my hometown," Lisa explains. "So I joined. By the end of the program a few months later, I'd lost 50 pounds. I looked great and felt even better. But even then, I had already gone back to some of the habits that had gotten me in trouble before. I was 'saving calories' so I could eat more at another meal and edging over the calorie limit— planning to make up the difference the next day."

Lisa started her junior year at North Carolina State thin and lovely. She attracted the attention of a fifth-year senior who asked her out. They dated seriously for three months before Lisa's Christian convictions, and his lack of them, created a permanent rift.

Devastated by the breakup, Lisa gained 20 pounds in three weeks. She comforted herself with two dozen doughnuts at one time. For lunch she'd order from one fast food restaurant and eat while driving to the second. Her grades plummeted as depression touched every area of her life.

By the end of the summer Lisa was suicidal. Curled up on her bed, she decided never to leave her room. Never to eat. Simply to die. Her mother helped her through the crisis and motivated her to live.

"By my senior year in college," Lisa recalls, "I had begun to seriously seek God and put Him first in my life. My parents had called their friends, Kenneth and Gloria Copeland, to ask for prayer for me. And with the help of one of their staff members, I'd begun praying in the Spirit every day, spending 30 minutes in the Word and listening to faith tapes daily. But, even so, I was still trying to diet and all I could think was, *I want to be thin!*"

Lisa's nightmarish cycle of diet and binge, lose and gain continued until, a year and a half later, her desperation drove her more deeply than ever into the Word of God.

"I started listening to tapes in all my free time," she says. "I listened to Kenneth and Gloria Copeland, Jesse Duplantis and Myles Munroe. I watched old movies that were inspirational and showed people overcoming. My weight was up to 200 pounds, but I had more peace. As I became more intimate with God, I learned to love and accept myself."

Then one day in August 1992, the breakthrough came.

Listening to praise tapes while she exercised, Lisa heard the Lord speak to her heart. *Lisa, you are doing so much with the Word, but you need to CHOOSE God or food. Really, the choice is God or Satan. You've been trying to have them both and it's made you double-minded!*

Opening her Bible, Lisa read the scripture in Deuteronomy 30:19, *"I call Heaven and earth to witness this day against you, that I have set before you life and death, the blessing and the curse; therefore choose life..." (The Amplified Bible).*

She couldn't deny that her food addiction was killing her. And the Bible said it was Satan who steals, kills and destroys (John 10:10). Certainly, her health and vitality had been stolen and her peace of mind destroyed.

Suddenly Lisa saw something about herself she'd never seen before. When she had made Jesus the Lord of her life at age 13, she'd failed to make Him Lord of her appetite.

The choice He was asking her to make now couldn't be more clear. Would she be willing to let Him choose what she would eat and when? Could she let Him be Lord of *all* her life? As she pondered the question, Romans 12:1 took on new meaning. *"Present your bodies a living* sacrifice...."

"Making that decision was the hardest thing I've ever done," Lisa says. "finally, in October of 1992, I said out loud, 'Okay, I choose God!' Then I prayed. I said, 'Lord, I'm going to live totally by Your direction and Your power instead of by my emotions. I won't be like an alcoholic who says, once an alcoholic, always an alcoholic. I admit I've spent nine years drunk on food. But I repent and ask Your forgiveness. I believe Your Word. I believe I can live free. I will never eat for my emotions again.'"

That day, Lisa King entered a battle for her life. She began every day saying what God's Word said about her. She never said another negative word about her weight or health. She confessed that she was free of food addictions, not because she *felt* free, but because God said she could live free. She confessed that she was lean and healthy and that she desired the food her body needed for nutrition.

When pressures mounted and the devil taunted her with thoughts of food, Lisa made herself pick up her Bible and read it out loud. "I didn't want to do it," she recalls. "I wanted to pick up a doughnut or a cookie or anything to eat. But I forced myself to read 2 Corinthians 10:5 and take captive thousands of thoughts about food as they bombarded me."

Sometimes, Lisa felt so exhausted from the battle, she'd have to take a nap. Other times, she'd play tapes by the Copelands when the temptation was tough. When her emotions were raging, Lisa put on praise tapes. When everything in her screamed for food she didn't need, she'd rejoice.

"I used to jump up and down shouting and rejoicing that I was free of my food addiction," Lisa remembers. "I'd be thinking, *I can't believe Lisa King is doing this!*"

Five months passed as Lisa held fast to her decision to choose God over food. When she made a mistake, she quickly repented and didn't allow any room for self-condemnation.

"Then suddenly, men started calling to ask me out," Lisa says. "The Holy Spirit showed me it was a trap. He revealed to me that in the past, I'd needed external attention so much I had focused more on outward appearance than on inward growth. The men I had dated were just one more way of getting that external attention."

When Satan couldn't trip Lisa through relationships anymore, he tried one last ploy. A physical injury. Once again the Holy Spirit showed her the trap. She guarded her confession, prayed, and received supernatural healing.

When the third tempting was finished, Lisa King knew she was free.

It's been over a year since Lisa gave her whole life—appetite and all—to God. And in that year, healthy eating has ceased to be a battle and become instead a joyous way of life.

"God has so changed my desires, I don't even like the same foods. I don't like the taste of pizza, and doughnuts make me sick. Most of my diet is raw fruits and vegetables. They taste so good!"

For years, Lisa's father joked about taking her shopping on Rodeo Drive in Hollywood. This year, he booked the trip. "Dad insisted that I needed new clothes," Lisa says, "and I did. I'd been wearing my mother's and sister's clothes, because all of mine were too big. I didn't need new clothes to reward myself for my progress. I already had my reward—a lean, healthy body. But the trip with dad sounded fun."

As the limo turned onto Rodeo Drive and pulled over in front of an exclusive shop selling Georgio Armani designs, Lisa's father helped her from the car and escorted her into the store.

Lisa selected a black after-five outfit and stepped into the dressing room. While they waited, her dad told the sales clerk, Wendy, something of Lisa's long struggle.

In the dressing room, Lisa stepped into the long, flowing skirt. She pulled the zipper up around her tiny waist. Then glanced in the mirror—and froze at the reflection.

It took a moment for Lisa to realize that she was the person in the mirror. She looked at herself, the person who'd been trapped for so long inside a prison of her own making, and burst into tears.

"Finally, I wiped my eyes and stepped out of the dressing room," Lisa recalls. "Dad and Wendy took one look at me and they both began to cry."

"I'm free," she said. "I'm free."

And Lisa King will be the first to tell you, whom the Son sets free is free indeed.

Update: The year after publishing Lisa's testimony, she went through some trials regarding her freedom. As Lisa put it, "Satan tried to bombard me with deception...but I have regained that victory." The Lord has reaffirmed to Lisa in a personal way that He looks on the heart, and that's where freedom begins. She wants people to know that it's only when we are grounded in the Word, see ourselves as God does, and stop trying to live up to man's expectations, that we are free.

Lisa has been a Partner with Kenneth Copeland Ministries for 9 years!

Climbing the Mountain

by Melanie Hemry

Bill Grier stumbled out of the church office with grief knotted in his stomach like a fist. If he heard one more pat answer to his problem he thought he'd scream. He didn't need pat answers. He needed help. Real help. And he didn't know where to find it. Bill Grier was homosexual.

He'd been counseled enough to understand *why* he had the problem. He'd been raised in a hopelessly dysfunctional family by an alcoholic father and mother in poor health. He'd suffered repeated rejections by his father. He'd been molested as a child. In fact, child molestation had plagued his family for several generations. His own grandmother had tried to kill him in the womb by hitting his mother's protruding belly with a fireplace poker. He *knew* all that. What he didn't know was *how* to overcome not only that past, but also the thoughts and desires that plagued him now.

Where had his life gone? Here he was in his 40s. He'd expected to be comfortable and secure by now. What did he have to show for his time on earth? Two failed marriages, four children he hardly knew, and a lifestyle of gay bars. A lifestyle he despised.

Sometimes his life seemed like a bad nightmare. Maybe if he pinched himself really hard he'd wake up and be 20 years old again—newly saved, newly Spirit filled and ordained as a minister of the gospel. Back then, in 1960, new converts weren't discipled. They just waded into the ministry with youthful zeal.

He had preached, pastored and evangelized. Those were the days when Bill Grier thought he had the answer to the world's problems. Now, 20 years later, he was face to face with the reality that he didn't even have the answer to his own problems.

"I was miserable," Bill says. "For 12 years I'd lived a lifestyle that I knew was sinful. I couldn't pretend it was anything else. I had received prayer. People had laid hands on me and cast out demonic spirits. But I wasn't free.

"In gay bars I met a lot of people who had been raised in Christian homes. I wasn't the only one who didn't know how to live victoriously over the sin of homosexuality. Ironically, the man I lived with also had been a minister.

On their second date, Bill told Barbara about his past. From that day on they spent hours together talking each day about the Lord and His plans. On October 20, 1989, they were married.

"There's nothing more miserable than being a Christian and living outside of the will of God. I was under constant conviction about my sin, yet I felt hopeless about how to change. I drank vodka to cope—a half gallon of vodka each week."

Eventually, Bill and his roommate, both desiring to find help in God, started attending church. One Saturday when Bill was going to buy vodka, he heard a voice he recognized—the voice of the Holy Spirit.

There's no point in buying that vodka, the Lord told him. *You're not going to drink it.*

Instead of his usual large supply, Bill bought only one bottle. Strangely, the next morning he didn't take a drink before church. That morning, both men rededicated their lives to God. They didn't just decide to *try* it God's way. They made a firm commitment. They trusted God with their sexuality. They trusted Him with their alcoholism. They trusted Him with their minds and emotions. They trusted Him with their lives.

"I made a decision," Bill recalls, "that sink, swim, live or die, I was going to serve God."

One gut-wrenching, teeth-clenching month later the two men poured that last bottle of vodka down the drain. The decision to obey God at all costs had paid off. Bill had gone from drinking a half gallon of vodka a week to zero alcohol consumption...with no symptoms of withdrawal. That assured him of one crucial fact—God was with him.

"I discovered that there was only one way to deal with this sin," Bill explains, "and that was through a no-compromise stance. I simply knew that if I compromised, I'd fall. It was too risky."

Bill was determined to follow God by faith. He began attending Full Gospel Business Men's meetings. It was at one of those meetings that he met Barbara.

"I seemed to run into Bill Grier everywhere I went," Barbara recalls. "I saw him at church. I saw him at Full Gospel Business Men's meetings. If I went to a special service somewhere he was there. He had a tremendous zeal and fervor for God.

"As our friendship grew, I—as a widow—was saying I would never marry again. But the Lord corrected me. *Don't say that.* He warned. *You don't know what My plans are.*

"I had heard a talk show discussing homosexuality. A man phoned in to share his experience. He didn't identify himself, but I recognized his voice. It was Bill. I prayed and asked God how I should respond if Bill told me about his past. The Lord said, *It's not going to change anything because Bill's past is forgiven. It's gone."*

On their second date, Bill told Barbara about his past. From that day on they spent hours together talking each day about the Lord and His plans. On October 20, 1989, they were married.

"The first help I ever received," Bill adds, "except through the Holy Spirit, was from a book. I started studying it on my own and reached a point where I knew I needed help beyond what it could give me. It wasn't so much the struggle over desire that made me seek help as dealing with the *cause*.

"Once as a young Christian, when I'd fallen into homosexual sin very briefly, I repented, fasted, prayed and went on to the mission field. But I didn't understand then that beginning with the molestation I'd experienced as a child, Satan had been building a nest in me. That nest needed to be cleaned out. I needed the Repairer of the Breach to heal my inner man."

Bill found a group of people who worked with others overcoming the sin of homosexuality. With their help he experienced some inner healing, and for a time, attended support group meetings.

"After a while," Bill remembers, "the Holy Spirit pulled me away from the group. He cautioned me against dwelling too much on the past, and warned me not to discuss those sins in detail because it would not glorify Him."

But the Holy Spirit did not leave Bill comfortless. Instead, He began teaching him from Genesis 19 about God rescuing Lot from Sodom and Gomorrah, the city destroyed because of homosexuality. In verses 15-17 he read:

And when the morning arose, then the angels hastened Lot, saying, Arise, take thy wife, and thy two daughters, which are here; lest thou be consumed in the iniquity of the city. And while he lingered, the men laid hold upon his hand, and upon the hand of his wife, and upon the hand of his two daughters; the Lord being merciful unto him: and they brought him forth, and set him without the city. And it came to pass, when they had brought them forth abroad, that he said, Escape for thy life; look not behind thee, neither stay thou in all the plain; escape to the mountain, lest thou be consumed.

"The Lord opened the scripture to me so that I could understand," Bill explains. "First, He showed me Lot lingered even though he knew the city was going to be destroyed. But the angels didn't just *tell* him to leave. They took him by the hand and led him out. He showed me that when Lot was directed to go to the mountain, it was fear that caused him to compromise.

"When God showed me that the angels wanted to lead Lot to the mountain, God's message was the same for me as it had been for him. God was saying, *Escape for your life! Don't look back, and don't stay anywhere in the valley.* He showed me that if I would put aside my own fear, He would take my hand and lead me out of the valley too. It was a message of no compromise. Lot asked to go only as far as the little city, but God's best was the mountain. The mountain represents the high calling of God in Christ Jesus."

Bill determined to follow that scriptural example and climb the mountain by faith.

"One of the most difficult things about coming out of

the homosexual lifestyle," Bill explains, "is the battle for the mind. Not only are there memories to deal with, but also pornography is an integral part of the homosexual culture. It took a long time to get rid of the memories of some of the filth I'd seen and read and heard."

The battle for the mind and memories seemed an uphill climb until Bill found the secret to success in Psalm 119:11: *"Thy word have I hid in mine heart, that I might not sin against thee."*

Bill discovered that there is only one way to cleanse the mind of filth—to wash it out with the Word of God. It was through this continual, cleansing process that his mind and heart were filled with truth and liberty.

"One of the first things Barbara shared with me was her collection of tapes by Kenneth and Gloria Copeland," Bill says. "Although there is no one person responsible for my freedom from homosexuality except the Holy Spirit, there was one person who finally discipled me: Kenneth Copeland. He taught a no-compromise message with more emphasis on the Word of God than any preacher I'd ever heard. His teaching gave me a leg to stand on, and gave me food for my spirit and soul."

It was that same teaching, adds Barbara, that has helped them build a wonderful marriage. "We used the principles Kenneth Copeland outlined in his book, *A Ceremony of Marriage* at our wedding," she says. "What's more, we live out those covenant principles. As a result, Bill and I are one in every way."

The tenderness in Barbara's voice makes it clear that she treasures that unity—and the victories God has given them—more than she can express.

"I knew the Lord had a call on Bill's life before I married him," she says. "God told me that Bill was His precious gem—a diamond. He said that a diamond doesn't shine in darkness. Only when the light reflects on it can you see the brilliance."

Today, Bill Grier's life reflects that brilliance. He will be the first to tell you that whenever you find yourself in a valley of temptation, if you'll reach your hand to Jesus, He'll lead you to the mountain. And the mountain is worth the climb.

Editor's Note: Today, Bill's former roommate is also free of homosexuality and living victoriously in the Lord.

Barbara has been a Partner with Kenneth Copeland Ministries for 16 years! And **Bill** became a Partner when he and Barbara married 7 years ago!

Prayer for Salvation
and Baptism in the Holy Spirit

Heavenly Father, I come to You in the Name of Jesus. Your Word says, *"...whosoever shall call on the name of the Lord shall be saved"* (Acts 2:21). I am calling on You. I pray and ask Jesus to come into my heart and be Lord over my life according to Romans 10:9-10. *"If thou shalt confess with thy mouth the Lord Jesus, and shalt believe in thine heart that God hath raised him from the dead, thou shalt be saved."* I do that now. I confess that Jesus is Lord, and I believe in my heart that God raised Him from the dead.

I am now reborn! I am a Christian—a child of Almighty God! I am saved! You also said in Your Word, *"If ye then, being evil, know how to give good gifts unto your children: HOW MUCH MORE shall your heavenly Father give the Holy Spirit to them that ask him?"* (Luke 11:13). I'm also asking You to fill me with the Holy Spirit. Holy Spirit, rise up within me as I praise God. I fully expect to speak with other tongues as You give me the utterance (Acts 2:4).

Begin to praise God for filling you with the Holy Spirit. Speak those words and syllables you receive—not in your own language, but the language given to you by the Holy Spirit. You have to use your own voice. God will not force you to speak.

Now you are a Spirit-filled believer. Continue with the blessing God has given you and pray in tongues each day. You'll never be the same!

Find a good Word of God preaching church, and become a part of a church family who will love and care for you as you love and care for them.

We need to be hooked up to each other. It increases our strength in God. It's God's plan for us.

Books by Kenneth Copeland

*   A Ceremony of Marriage
     A Matter of Choice
     Covenant of Blood
     Faith and Patience—The Power Twins
*   Freedom From Fear
     From Faith to Faith—A Daily Guide to Victory
     Giving and Receiving
     Healing Promises
     Honor Walking in Honesty, Truth & Integrity
     How to Conquer Strife
     How to Discipline Your Flesh
     How to Receive Communion
     Love Never Fails
*   Now Are We in Christ Jesus
*   Our Covenant With God
*   Prayer—Your Foundation for Success
     Prosperity Promises
     Prosperity: The Choice Is Yours
     Rumors of War
*   Sensitivity of Heart
     Six Steps to Excellence in Ministry
     Sorrow Not! Winning Over Grief and Sorrow
*   The Decision Is Yours
*   The Force of Faith
*   The Force of Righteousness
     The Image of God in You
     The Laws of Prosperity
*   The Mercy of God
     The Miraculous Realm of God's Love
     The Outpouring of the Spirit—The Result of Prayer
     The Power of the Tongue
     The Power to Be Forever Free
     The Troublemaker
     The Winning Attitude
*   Welcome to the Family
*   You Are Healed!
     Your Right-Standing With God

*Available in Spanish

Books by Kenneth Copeland

Books by Gloria Copeland

*   And Jesus Healed Them All
Are You Ready?
Build Yourself an Ark
From Faith to Faith—A Daily Guide to Victory
God's Success Formula
*   God's Will for You
God's Will for Your Healing
God's Will Is Prosperity
God's Will Is the Holy Spirit
Harvest of Health
Healing Promises
Love—The Secret to Your Success
No Deposit—No Return
Pressing In—It's Worth It All
The Power to Live a New Life
The Unbeatable Spirit of Faith
*   Walk in the Spirit
Walk With God
Well Worth the Wait

*Available in Spanish

Other Books Published by KCP

Heirs Together by Mac Hammond
John G. Lake—His Life, His Sermons, His Boldness of Faith
Winning the World by Mac Hammond

World Offices of
Kenneth Copeland Ministries

For more information about KCM and a free catalog, please write the office nearest you:

Kenneth Copeland Ministries
Fort Worth, Texas 76192-0001

Kenneth Copeland
Locked Bag 2600
Mansfield Delivery Centre
QUEENSLAND 4122
AUSTRALIA

Kenneth Copeland
Post Office Box 15
BATH
BA1 1GD
ENGLAND

Kenneth Copeland
Post Office Box 830
RANDBURG
2125
REPUBLIC OF SOUTH AFRICA

Kenneth Copeland
Post Office Box 58248
Vancouver
BRITISH COLUMBIA
V6P 6K1
CANADA

220123 MINSK
REPUBLIC OF BELARUS
Post Office 123
P/B 35
Kenneth Copeland Ministries